A PRAGMATIC GUIDE TO COMPETENCY
Tools, Frameworks and Assessment

BCS THE CHARTERED INSTITUTE FOR IT

Our mission as BCS, The Chartered Institute for IT, is to enable the information society. We promote wider social and economic progress through the advancement of information technology science and practice. We bring together industry, academics, practitioners and government to share knowledge, promote new thinking, inform the design of new curricula, shape public policy and inform the public.

Our vision is to be a world-class organisation for IT. Our 70,000 strong membership includes practitioners, businesses, academics and students in the UK and internationally. We deliver a range of professional development tools for practitioners and employees. A leading IT qualification body, we offer a range of widely recognised qualifications.

Further Information
BCS, The Chartered Institute for IT,
First Floor, Block D,
North Star House, North Star Avenue,
Swindon, SN2 1FA, United Kingdom.
T +44 (0) 1793 417 424
F +44 (0) 1793 417 444
www.bcs.org/contactus

A PRAGMATIC GUIDE TO COMPETENCY

Tools, Frameworks and Assessment

Jon Holt and Simon Perry

Published by British Informatics Society Limited (BISL), a wholly owned subsidiary of BCS, The Chartered Institute for IT, First Floor, Block D, North Star House, North Star Avenue, Swindon, SN2 1FA, UK. www.bcs.org

ISBN 978-1-906124-70-0

British Cataloguing in Publication Data.
A CIP catalogue record for this book is available at the British Library.

Typeset by Lapiz Digital Services, Chennai, India.
Printed at CPI Antony Rowe, Chippenham and Eastbourne, UK.

This book is dedicated to Mike, my mentor, friend and paragon of competence
JDH

To Stu, Jo and Sue, probably the best siblings in the world
SAP

CONTENTS

LIST OF FIGURES AND TABLES

AUTHORS

Dr Jon Holt is an international award-winning author and public speaker in the field of applied systems engineering and research. He has authored many books and papers on systems engineering. His books cover the application of UML and SysML to systems engineering, process modelling, enterprise architectures and competency assessment.

Jon is active in the IET (the Institution of Engineering and Technology) via their Professional Networks and in BCS, the Chartered Institute for IT, as a member of the Learned Society. He is a Fellow of both the IET and BCS and is a Chartered Engineer and Chartered IT Professional.

Jon was the founder-director of Brass Bullet Ltd, a systems engineering consultancy and training company for over 12 years, until it was acquired in 2009. He is currently the Global Head of Systems Engineering for Atego, the leading independent provider of tools and capability for systems engineering.

Simon Perry has worked as a software engineer, systems architect and systems engineer for over 20 years in a wide range of business areas including defence, finance, building construction, nuclear installations, utilities and transport.

Simon is a Principal Consultant at Atego where his role includes consulting, mentoring and the development and delivery of training courses. His main areas of work are concerned with the application of systems modeling to all aspects of systems engineering: process modeling, enterprise architectures and architectural frameworks, requirements engineering, capabilities and competencies.

Simon is a visiting lecturer at Warwick University where he teaches a software engineering course to third year students.

He is the co-author, with Jon Holt, of two other books on modeling and systems engineering. Simon is a member of a number of professional bodies: INCOSE, the IET and BCS. He regularly speaks at events organised by these bodies.

ACKNOWLEDGEMENTS

Unprovided with original learning, unformed in the habits of thinking, unskilled in the arts of composition, I resolved to write a book
Edward Gibbon

As with all my work, none of it could be possible without the help of many people.

We had lots of help with carrying out the competency assessments, with many people being prepared to let them loose either on themselves or their staff. A big thanks to Alan in Cardiff and his staff who we assessed and subsequently published with – it was a pleasure to work with you! The usual suspects from Aldermaston also deserve a lot of thanks, including Duncan, Jon, Nicky and Keith. Extra thanks go to P3mby who, as usual, went the extra mile and produced some lovely additional work for us – if only they gave out Doctorates for spreadsheets! All the good folk at Abbey Wood should be thanked, including Dave, all of his staff and the many assessees. In terms of helping us perform many, many assessments, special thanks go to Rick, Emma, Tony and Dave from Shrivenham who helped us put the process through the wringer and refine it into what we have today. In terms of innovation, dedication and the sheer volume of work done to tailor the whole approach, we must thank Sylvia who did more for the process and its application than she could ever know. It's Sylvia's work that gave us the confidence that we could apply the approach in just about any area imaginable and for this, we take our collective hats off to you.

Thanks to all the good folk at the now-no-longer Brass Bullet Ltd and, more recently, all my new colleagues at Atego. Special thanks to Simon and Mikey B – I am blessed to still be working with both of them after all these years, and look forward to many more.

Of course, thanks as ever go to Mike and Sue. I continue to be inspired by both of them and have learned recently from Sue that 'it's never too late' to keep striving for self-improvement in life.

Finally, all my love and thanks to my beautiful wife, Rebecca, my three (generally) wonderful children, Jude, Eliza and Roo, and my two cats Olive-the-Wondercat and Betty-Moose Davies.

Jon Holt, January 2011

As Jon has said, this book would not have been possible without the help of many people and organisations that worked with Jon and me to develop the UCAM and helped us clarify the approach. I therefore echo Jon's thanks to them all. I would also like to extend my thanks to all those INCOSE members who helped develop the INCOSE Systems Engineering Competencies Framework, and in particular those that I had the pleasure to work with on the Phase 3 Working Group, particularly Simon, Richard, Sandra, David, Dez, Jocelyn, Shane and Ady.

Finally, I could not have written this book and kept my sanity without the love, encouragement and support of my wife Sally. She continues to inspire me every day, and is the only person I know who would put up with being woken by my enthusiastic bongo playing with such equanimity. Also, thanks to our feline alarm clock, Motley the cat, who never fails to wake me up at all the wrong times.

Simon Perry, January 2011

PREFACE

Recent years have seen a significant increase in the use of personnel competency assessments within organisations. This trend derives from the understanding that a well-executed competency assessment programme can offer many and various benefits. A competency assessment programme, for example, can be used in the enhancement of:

- 'best fit' human resource allocation;
- professional development of employees;
- pay review processes;
- training requirements identification;
- customer assurance in tendering;
- ability to realize organisational capability.

If however a competency assessment programme is not well executed, if its implementation is **ad hoc,** then, like all powerful tools in ill-prepared hands, it can cause immense damage and all the areas of potential benefit could actually be adversely affected in the process.

Competency is a measure of an individual's ability in terms of their knowledge, skills and behaviour to perform a given role. Competency assessment in an organisation, if carried out correctly, will be key to the organisation's overall capability improvement and will lead to improved customer confidence. To be correct a competency assessment process must be:

- repeatable, so that comparison of results can be made;
- measurable, in measures that are documented, known and understood;
- based on best practice, traceable to standards and frameworks;
- transferable between frameworks, as an assessment process limited to a single framework will have limited application;
- tailorable, so that it can be modified for different organisations or for different sections within a single organisation.

This book defines an approach and a set of processes for competency assessment that satisfy these criteria – a set of powerful tools that can be used by an organisation to consolidate its competency assessment work into a coherent approach, allowing assessments against competencies from multiple frameworks to be undertaken.

1   INTRODUCTION

The incompetent with nothing to do can still make a mess of it
Laurence J Peter

In order to succeed in any business, conventional wisdom tells us that we need three things: people, process and products. We need people with the right skills to do their jobs properly, we need processes in place in order to realise and demonstrate our capabilities and we need the right products, or tools, to allow us to do our jobs properly. This book is about people. In particular, this book is about demonstrating how professional we are as people and about inspiring confidence in those around us.

Confidence is a commodity that is none too easy to quantify, yet one that drives a lot of what we do in everyday life. Whenever we buy a product or service, we need to have confidence that it will do its job properly. Whenever we deal with a person on an individual level, it is important that we have confidence in them – likewise, it is also important that others have confidence in us. In order to inspire confidence, it is essential that we can demonstrate our own professionalism, which comes down to our individual competence. This competence may take many forms, for example, technical knowledge, qualifications, presentation skills, peer recognition, social skills and so on. But what are these competences and how do we demonstrate them to other people? This books aims to cover exactly that – how to decide what competencies are relevant and how to demonstrate our own, or assess others', competencies.

There is, undoubtedly, an overhead in implementing the kind of robust, repeatable and rigorous approach to competency assessment described in this book. So why bother? Why is demonstrating professionalism and inspiring confidence so important if it adds to an organisation's overheads? The simple answer is another question: what is the cost of failure if you **don't** demonstrate professionalism and inspire confidence?

It is very easy for projects to go wrong. When projects do go wrong and result in disasters or failures, then they will inevitably become big news. When projects go well, on the other hand, they are ignored. The reality of this unfortunate state of affairs is that clients' confidence is damaged and the whole issue of professionalism is brought into question.

This can have a serious impact on an organisation, with a direct loss of income resulting from failure, a drop in share prices and, perhaps more importantly, damage to an organisation's reputation that can take years to restore, all being possible outcomes for the organisation. Witness, for example, the massive cost, drop in share value and damage to reputation of BP resulting from the Gulf of Mexico oil spill in 2010. It is estimated that the spill will cost the company $40 billion. Following the spill, it was reported that BP's shares had fallen by 35 per cent resulting in a $60 billion loss in market value and that there had been a 10 to 40 per cent drop in petrol sales in the USA.

Being able to demonstrate professionalism and inspire confidence can help to avoid such costly failure. It can also be an important differentiator that can help to distinguish one organisation from another and can, perhaps, make the difference between winning and losing a contract.

Before we go further, it is important that there are some clear definitions for the key terms that will be used throughout this book. The terms used are very similar and, therefore, it is crucial that they are defined at this point and that the subtle differences in meaning are pointed out. The terms used in this book are taken from the Cambridge English dictionary and are:

- competence – the ability to do something well;
- competency – an important skill that is needed to do a job.

The key difference here is that 'competence' reflects the total ability of the individual, whereas a 'competency' is a single skill; (hopefully) one of many that the individual will hold. The sum of an individual's competencies will make up their competence and it is these individual competencies that are assessed to provide an overall indication of competence.

COMPETENCY ASSESSMENT

In order to demonstrate competence, there must be some way to qualify and measure it, and this is where competency assessment comes in. Competency assessment may take many forms, from filling in a simple form to in-depth psychological analysis, and any, or all, of these techniques may be valid where appropriate. This book proposes a process-based approach to competency assessment known as the Universal Competency Assessment Model that is intended to be as flexible and scalable as possible.

There are several reasons why someone may want to carry out a competency assessment:

- To inspire customer confidence and provide a competitive edge. This was alluded to in the previous section, but what this comes down to is our own credibility, and the confidence that this will inspire in others. When someone makes a choice between a number of people to do something, it is the one who inspires the most confidence who will usually be chosen. One initial argument against this statement is that cost will often have an impact, as some people will always go for the cheapest option but, to counter this, people will also pay more for someone in whom they have confidence. Therefore, on a purely financial level, demonstrating competence is one way to charge more for a person and can be used to help strengthen a business case for someone to pay more money.

- As part of an individual's career development, at a professional or personal level. At a professional level this may include being formally recognised by our peers or by a professional body. For example, achieving 'chartered' status is seen as a goal in many industries and will often be accompanied by a right to practise in a particular field. Indeed, in many areas, a certain level of formal competence is necessary in order to work. On a personal level, many people are interested in planning their career paths and setting themselves individual goals. This may be, for example, obtaining chartered status or gaining a new position in an organisation. Again, competency assessment can be used as a valuable tool when developing a career plan or carrying out Continued Professional Development (CPD).

- As part of a recruitment process. Many organisations are finding that recruiting people on the basis of a CV (resumé) or a single interview is simply not good enough. It is all too easy to be impressed by someone's CV or the way that they perform at an interview, only to be let down when they actually start the work. Many organisations now use competency assessment not just as an added measure but as a major part of the actual recruitment process itself. We are living in an increasingly litigious world and it is very difficult to remove someone from a company without long and costly lawsuits (which can put a small company out of business) so it becomes even more important that we recruit the right people in the first instance.

- As part of an organisation's appraisal process. Most companies carry out some sort of appraisal on a regular basis. For example, it may be that each person in a company is assessed on an annual basis to see if they are performing properly. Competency assessment can be a very powerful tool in such cases, as it allows competencies that people possess to be compared directly to the competencies required for their post. It is a very useful mechanism to have a competency set (known as a 'competency scope') defined for different positions in the business, as it is then possible to compare people's actual competencies (known as a 'competency profile') with the competency scope to assess suitability. By comparing several of these competency profiles, it is also possible to see how a person's competence has evolved over time and how quickly. This can give an excellent indication of the ability and willingness of a person to learn and take on new tasks. Such competency assessments are being used widely for appraisal and even, in some cases, being tied directly into pay reviews.

- To identify training requirements from the point of view of a person or business unit. It is essential that people have the right competencies for their job and when gaps have been identified through assessment, this can be used as an excellent guide in those areas for which training is required. This can be done at a personal level for personal development or may be done as part of a team or business unit effort.

- To identify training requirements from a trainer's point of view. Competency frameworks and competency assessments are big news for training providers – or should be. By understanding those areas in which people require competence and how they will be assessed, it is possible to create new courses and tailor existing courses towards delivering these competencies. A good training course should map onto established and recognised competency frameworks so that the people buying the training know exactly what they are getting and can map it directly onto their business plans. This not only provides a better service, but also provides another good reason why someone should choose you as a trainer over your competitors.

These are not the only reasons why competency assessment is so important, but it should provide an indication of some of the main reasons why we need to understand and be able to demonstrate competence.

When considering the whole idea of competency assessment, it is essential that you consider why you want to do it in the first place, and what you want to achieve. In the world of engineering, this is known as establishing the require-ments for a system or project and it is very important that this is not taken lightly, as too many people will blindly apply competency assessment to their work and not understand why. Unsurprisingly, these are often the same people that cannot see the point of competency assessment and see it as an unnecessary overhead.

PEOPLE'S PERCEPTIONS OF THEIR OWN COMPETENCE

Every person has their own opinion of how competent they are in a particular area, regardless of how competent they actually are. In their fascinating paper on people's own views of themselves, Kruger and Dunning (1999) ran a series of four trials where they asked a sample of people to judge how competent they saw themselves being. The results of this work were quite surprising as it demon-strated that incompetent people tend to see themselves as more competent than they actually are, whereas more competent people tend to see themselves as less competent than they actually are. The authors summed this up quite nicely by stating

> people who are unskilled in these domains suffer a dual burden: not only do these people reach erroneous conclusions and make unfortunate choices, but their incompetence robs them of the metacognitive ability to realize it.

This is very important as it means that the incompetent will rate themselves higher, whereas competent people will rate themselves lower. One of the dangers here is that two people may each rate themselves and come to the same conclusion – that they hold a certain level of competence. The truth may be, however, that they are both at opposite ends of the competence spectrum, but that people may think that they are the same.

This can have a direct impact on an organisation, since it means that less competent people can be undertaking work for which they are not competent, possibly leading to work that is not fit for purpose and which costs the organisation both time and money to put right and, perhaps more importantly, adversely affects their reputation. Conversely, the more competent person may be given work that is below their level of competency. This also constrains the performance of an organisation, since it is not making the best use of that person.

This is a crucial reason why there is such a need for a pragmatic approach to competency assessment that can minimise the chance of these errors occurring. The assessments should be as objective as possible and, of course, the competency of the assessors themselves should be brought into question.

One of the conclusions made by the authors of this excellent paper is that incompetent people have no idea how incompetent they are, a conclusion that has been backed up by many previous studies referenced in the paper. The use of competency assessment, with a good, simple visual output may go some way to convincing incompetent people that they do not hold the lofty levels of competence that they believe that they do.

COMPETENCE VERSUS CAPABILITY

There is often some confusion between the terms 'capability' and 'competence' as they are inherently very closely related to each other. However, there are subtle differences between the two, so, for the purposes of this book, the definitions will be as follows:

- Capability describes the ability of an organisation or organisational unit.
- Competence describes the ability of an individual to do something.

When we talk about capability in the sense defined here, we are talking about the ability to deliver a product or service. This ability is demonstrated through the use of effective processes. Indeed, when it comes to assessing capability, the established approach is to assess the process which provides an indication of the capability and its maturity. Examples of such capability determination include: the Capability Maturity Model Integrated (CMMI) (and its family) and Software Process Improvement and Capability dEtermination (SPICE).

Capability has been an increasingly important subject over the last 10 years or so as many large project tenders are now awarded on the basis of capability. For example, as part of a tender, bidders will be asked not only to provide an overview of their solution but also will be asked to demonstrate that they have the capability to deliver that solution. One of the problems associated with such an approach is that capability can be demonstrated in an organisation, but in order to realise that capability, it is necessary to have staff with appropriate competence. Many large organisations will bid for projects without having enough staff to carry out the work and will then recruit new staff once they have won the contract. In many cases, this will involve employing people, known as contractors, on a contractual basis. Many contractors, as is the nature of the job, will change employers and projects, depending on where their skills are required. As a consequence of this, it is not unusual to find the same people working on different contracts depending on who has won what. This has the potential to have a very negative impact on a project as, in some cases, new contracts come up as the company responsible for delivering the previous contract has not done its job properly and will not be awarded another contract. If the people who have performed so badly on one contract then change employers and switch to the new project, has any benefit whatsoever been achieved?

As a result of this type of activity happening time and time again, companies are coming around to realising that not only is the capability important, but also the competencies of the staff needed to realise that capability.

It is possible to draw up a simple equation to represent this relationship – before immediately switching off at the very thought of an equation, please bear in mind that this is about as mathematically challenging as this book will get.

> Confidence = capability + competence

In order to inspire confidence, we need to **demonstrate** both the capability (ability of the business) and the competence (ability of the individuals). This demonstration is crucial in order to inspire confidence. It is no good simply having ways to define and measure capability and competence if they are never applied; confidence comes from the **active** demonstration of both capability and competence.

When we need to demonstrate capability, we need best-practice models against which to compare our processes, usually in the form of standards. When we need to demonstrate competence, we also need best-practice models, which are usually in the form of **competency frameworks.**

COMPETENCY FRAMEWORKS

A competency framework describes a set of competencies (the 'things' that are measured to demonstrate competence) that are applicable to a particular field. Every industry has some sort of competency framework, as do many organisations. These frameworks should be viewed as standards and, just like any other standard, they may exist at many levels, including:

- Generic frameworks, which may apply internationally and apply to a particular discipline.

- Industry-specific frameworks. Some industries have their own frameworks that are usually owned by relevant professional bodies or industrial organisations. Examples of these include, among others, Skills Framework for the Information Age (SFIA) for the IT industry and Association of Proposal Management Professionals (APMP) for the bidding industry.

- Organisation-specific frameworks. Many companies, particularly large ones, have their own competency framework that is geared towards their particular organisation. These frameworks are often held and managed by the human resources centre but in many cases, as is increasingly becoming the case, a dedicated role or department may be allocated specifically to address all matters relating to competency and competency assessment.

- Regulatory or legally required frameworks. Some industries have their own competency frameworks that actually become mandated as part of a certification scheme. For example, the railway industry in the UK has such a scheme for railway signalling. The Institution of Railway Signal Engineers (IRSE) operates a competence certification scheme, known as the 'IRSE Licensing Scheme'. To quote from their official website, the main aim of the scheme is

to provide assurance about the competence of individuals to carry out technical safety-critical or safety-related work on signalling and railway telecommunications equipment and systems. It provides a cross industry accepted benchmark of competence for personnel carrying out a range of activities from maintenance through design, installation, testing, project engineering and senior technical management.

The railway signalling industry is by no means unique and there are equivalent schemes in other industries, such as the nuclear and aerospace industries.

- Technique or technology-based frameworks. Some specific techniques have their own competence programmes that demonstrate an individual's knowledge and skills for that technique. For example, the Unified Modelling Language (UML) is a visual modelling language that is used extensively in the worlds of software and systems engineering. The language itself is specified in a standard that is managed and configured by a standards body known as the Object Management Group (OMG) in the USA. The management group operates a scheme known as the 'OMG Certified UML Professional', or OCUP, that is a 'rigorous, comprehensive, and fair test of a person's knowledge of OMG's specifications for unified modeling language' (OCUP).

A number of frameworks will be discussed later in this book, but for now consider the question of which framework is the right one for you. This is a question that is not quite so easily answered. For example, you may work in the Information Technology (IT) industry and use the SFIA framework as a basis for assessments. However, this framework is aimed mainly at the technical aspects of IT and not so much at the management side, so it may be that it is desirable also to look at the Association of Project Management (APM) framework also. Now consider the scenario where you may also be involved with bidding for IT projects, in which case another framework, such as APMP may also be of interest. What if there is also an in-house framework that needs to be used?

The point here is that each framework will have its own strengths and weaknesses, which is only natural and is certainly not intended to be a criticism of any particular framework. As a consequence of this, it is often required to mix-and-match between different frameworks in order to get the most appropriate parts of each and combine them into a single framework. However, this is far easier said than done and the issue of trying to use more than one framework is a very challenging and complex one.

The same problem occurs when one wants to create a new framework for a different industry. The last thing that the world needs is yet more frameworks, so, again, the idea of cherry-picking different parts from different frameworks is a very attractive one. This is one of the areas that this book will address.

EVOLUTION OF COMPETENCE OVER TIME

One of the most common misconceptions concerning competence is that the goal is to hold the highest competence possible and that an individual's competence should constantly increase as their career progresses. This is complete fallacy. The goal is to hold the appropriate competence for whatever role is being played. As an individual's career progresses, their role will, quite naturally, evolve. For example, someone may start their career as a technician and then move into a more senior technical role, then progress (or regress) to management, before ending up at board level in an organisation. The point here is that the competence for that person is not increasing all the time, but the role that they play is changing and, hence, the set of competencies that define their competence will change over time. It is important that the person holds the right competence for each role at each point in their career. This phenomenon will be referred to as 'competence evolution' and will become very important when competency profiles are discussed later in this book.

ASSESSMENT VERSUS AUDIT

When we talk about demonstrating competence, we inevitably use the phrase 'competency assessment'. This is no accident and it is very important that the term 'assessment' rather than 'audit' is used.

When the term 'audit' is used, it implies that there will be a binary outcome or, to put it another way, a 'pass or fail' outcome. A typical audit will identify a number of areas that are of interest, compare it to a standard and identify a set of non-conformances (usually major and minor). The result of such an audit will be a straight pass or fail, as a set of non-conformances will be provided.

When the term 'assessment' is used, it implies that there will be a graduated outcome that will provide an indication of a level of achievement in a particular area. The result of an assessment will typically be a profile that will show how mature a person (in the case of competency) or organisation (in the case of capability) is in a specific area. One of the major goals of an assessment approach is to provide a mechanism for self-improvement, and a profile, rather than a pass-or-fail output, is far more useful for this. This is a very simplified definition of an audit, but it is not within the scope of this book to argue the pros and cons of audits versus assessments, but it is useful to understand, at a high level, the differences between the two.

SCOPE OF THIS BOOK

This book is aimed at people who have an interest in understanding and defining competency frameworks. It is also aimed at people who may be interested in carrying out competency assessment, whether it is for self-assessment or third-party assessment. The book will show how a number of these frameworks work and how they can be understood and analysed. A process will also be introduced and described that can be used to assess competency using any framework. A number of real-world case studies will be described that show a number of different ways in which the processes and approach in this book can be applied in reality.

CONCLUSIONS

There is a need for inspiring confidence in the people with whom we deal, whether they are clients or fellow workers. In order to inspire confidence, we need to demonstrate our professionalism at an organisational and personal level. At an organisational level, we need to demonstrate capability and at a personal level, we need to demonstrate competence.

In order to demonstrate competence, there is a need for competency assessment that can be applied in a flexible and scalable manner. We demonstrate competency according to established and recognised norms, usually in the form of single, or a set of, competency frameworks. When using multiple frameworks, it is desirable to mix and match between them in order to ensure that the resultant framework is a good fit for our original requirements.

REFERENCES

Cambridge English Dictionary (CED)

Software Process Improvement and Capability dEtermination (SPICE). See ISO 15504 – Software process assessment suite of documents, parts 1 to 7 www.iso.org (Accessed February 2011).

Capability Maturity Model Integrated (CMMI) suite of documents, including: (2006) 'CMMI for Development, Version 1.2' (pdf). *CMMI-DEV (Version 1.2, August 2006).* Carnegie Mellon University Software Engineering Institute. www.sei.cmu.edu/library/abstracts/reports/06tr008.cfm (Accessed February 2011).

(2007) 'CMMI for Acquisition, Version 1.2' (pdf). *CMMI-ACQ (Version 1.2, November 2007).* Carnegie Mellon University Software Engineering Institute. www.sei.cmu.edu/library/abstracts/reports/07tr017.cfm (Accessed February 2011).

(2007) 'CMMI for Services, Version 1.2' (pdf). *CMMI-SVC (Version 1.2, February 2009).* Carnegie Mellon University Software Engineering Institute. www.sei.cmu.edu/library/abstracts/reports/09tr001.cfm (Accessed February 2011).

Institution for Railway Signal Engineers (IRSE) www.irse.org/Licensing.html (Accessed February 2011).

Kruger, J. and Dunning, D. (1999) Unskilled and unaware of it: how difficulties in recognising one's own incompetence lead to inflated self-assessment. *J Pers. Soc. Psychol.* Dec. 77 (6): 1121–1134.

Object Management Group (OCUP): www.omg.org/uml-certification/ (Accessed February 2011).

2 COMPETENCY FRAMEWORKS

Force has no place where there is need of skill
Herodotus

INTRODUCTION

This chapter looks at some of the many competency frameworks that exist in the real world. A small sample of these frameworks will be chosen and investigated in more detail. The main aim behind this exercise is to show the different structures of the frameworks and to discuss how each one achieves its stated objectives. There are two broad categories of frameworks that will be considered here, which are:

- Public-domain frameworks. These public domain frameworks are typically geared towards a specific industry or profession and are often managed and controlled by professional bodies or industry groups. Indeed, as will be discussed later in this book, one of the main uses for competency frameworks and competency assessment is for continued professional development, so it is natural that the professional bodies take a leading role in such matters.

- Private or in-house frameworks. These are typically geared specifically towards a particular organisation or company and are usually proprietary. As they are owned by their relevant organisations, these tend not to be available for the general public and tend to be used exclusively for in-house activities, such as staff appraisals, tendering, and so on.

For the purposes of this chapter, the focus will be solely on the public-domain frameworks and will not cover private frameworks at all. Having said that, the same concepts that are identified and discussed for public frameworks are equally applicable to private frameworks.

The sample of frameworks has been chosen to provide a wide spread of interest across a number of disciplines and, in particular, will include:

- UKSPEC, the UK Standard for Professional Engineering Competence. The UKSPEC is the cornerstone of all technical competences in the UK. The UKSPEC is used as the basis for professional accreditation, such as Chartered Engineer (CEng) and Chartered IT Professional (CITP), and all UK professional bodies use it as part of their professional assessment. The UKSPEC is owned and managed by the Engineering Council (see UKSPEC for more details);

- SFIA. The acronymically challenged framework known as SFIA (pronounced 'Sophia') is a framework that is geared towards the skills required for the effective implementation and use of Information Systems (ISs) making use of Information and Communications Technology (ICT). The SFIA framework maps directly back to the UKSPEC and is owned and managed by the SFIA Foundation (see SFIA for more details);

- INCOSE, the International Council on Systems Engineering competencies framework, is an international body that is committed to furthering the discipline of systems engineering. They have produced a competency framework that maps back to the UKSPEC and covers various cross-cutting concepts associated with systems engineering. Please note that the term 'systems engineering' is the engineering definition of the term, rather than the IT definition of the term. The INCOSE framework is owned and managed by INCOSE (see INCOSE for more details);

- APM, the Association for Project Management Body of Knowledge. The APM framework forms the heart of the APM assessment and accreditation and is aimed specifically at the discipline of project management for all industries. The APM Body of Knowledge is owned and managed by the APM (see APM for more details);

- APMP, the Association of Proposal Management Professionals framework. The APMP (not to be confused with APM) framework is aimed specifically at proposal and bid management within an organisation and identifies a number of skills required for such activities. The APMP framework is owned and managed by the APMP (see APMP for more details).

These particular frameworks were chosen as they represent a broad spread of interest and will hopefully provide, at a minimum, one that is directly related to most readers' professions. The idea here is to show that the techniques introduced and discussed in this book can be used for any framework and are not just limited to technical skills, but can be applied across the wider business.

In order to understand each framework and to get it into a format that can be compared and contrasted, each of the frameworks has been modelled in order to identify areas of complexity, aid understanding and help to communicate the different key concepts. The approach taken was the 'seven views' approach (Holt 2009) and uses the UML as its modelling notation. It should be stressed, however, before the readers of this book collectively snap it shut in disgust, that this is not a modelling book and it is not intended to provide a treatise on the pros and cons of modelling and its various notations. Please be assured that the modelling utilised in this book is used purely as a tool and will be kept to an absolute minimum.

The main use of the modelling in this chapter is to provide a brief, high-level ontology for each of the frameworks, so that the concepts may be compared and contrasted. These ontologies will also be used as a basis for abstracting a common ontology in the next chapter. Each ontology simply identifies the main concepts and terminology that is used in each framework and relates them together in the form of diagrams.

THE UKSPEC

Introduction

It was stated earlier that the UKSPEC is the cornerstone of all technical competences in the UK. The UKSPEC is used as the basis for professional accreditation, such as CEng and CITP, and all UK professional bodies use it as part of their professional assessment. It is essential, therefore, that the UKSPEC is understood before any other framework is looked at. To put matters bluntly, if a framework does not map onto the concepts in the UKSPEC, then it will not be recognised at a professional level.

The UKSPEC ontology

The UKSPEC, just like all the other frameworks, can be distilled down to a simple diagram that encapsulates all the main concepts, the terminology used and the relationships between them. In other words, it has a simple ontology.

Figure 2.1 Key concepts for UKSPEC

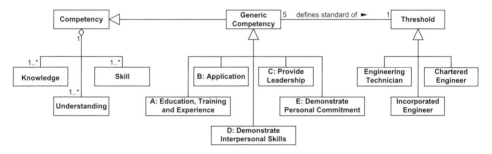

The diagram in Figure 2.1 shows the key concepts and terminology for the UKSPEC. It can be seen that 'Competency' is made up of the following concepts:

- 'Knowledge', which refers to having domain knowledge in a particular discipline or application area. For example, a university degree in engineering will provide a basic knowledge of engineering (the discipline) while experience in industry would also provide knowledge of the field (domain knowledge).

- 'Skill', which refers to the techniques, tools, methodologies and approaches that are employed in order to implement the knowledge. The skill depends upon having the knowledge in the first instance and really makes the knowledge useful, rather than knowledge for the sake of knowledge.

- 'Understanding', which refers to the ability to be able to apply the right knowledge and skills at the right time and to understand the implications for such use. This is the really difficult aspect of competence to get right. It involves understanding why the knowledge and skills have been employed and what benefits have been realised in doing so.

Competency may be thought of as existing in five 'Generic competency' categories, which are:

1. 'A: Education, training and experience'. This includes formal education, industrial training, work experience, and so on.

2. 'B: Application'. This includes being able to apply, or having experience of applying the different skills and knowledge for particular application areas.

3. 'C: Provide leadership'. It is important that an individual is able to lead teams or other individuals where necessary, which is reflected here.

4. 'D: Demonstrate interpersonal skills'. This includes what is often referred to as 'soft skills' such as verbal and non-verbal communication, abstract things, and so on.

5. 'E: Demonstrate personal commitment'. This includes embracing CPD, involvement with professional bodes and industrial groups, publishing, promoting engineering, and so on.

These competencies are held at a particular level or 'Threshold' and, currently, there are three levels of recognition within the Engineering Council UK (ECUK):

1. Engineering Technician (EngTech). The EngTech qualification defines the competence and commitment required before an individual can call themselves an engineering technician. The UKSPEC defines an engineering technician as someone who is

> concerned with applying proven techniques and procedures to the solution of practical engineering problems. They carry supervisory or technical responsibility, and are competent to exercise creative aptitudes and skills within defined fields of technology. Professional Engineering Technicians contribute to the design, development, manufacture, commissioning, decommissioning, operation or maintenance of products, equipment, processes or services. Professional Engineering Technicians are required to apply safe systems of working.

2. Incorporated Engineer (IEng). The IEng qualification defines the competence and commitment required before an individual can call themselves an incorporated engineer. The UKSPEC defines an incorporated engineer as someone who can

> maintain and manage applications of current and developing technology, and may undertake engineering design, development, manufacture, construction and operation. Incorporated Engineers are variously engaged in technical and commercial management and possess effective interpersonal skills.

3. Chartered Engineer (CEng). The CEng qualification defines the competence and commitment required before an individual can call themselves a chartered engineer. The UKSPEC defines a chartered engineer as someone who is

characterized by their ability to develop appropriate solutions to engineering problems, using new or existing technologies, through innovation, creativity and change. They might develop and apply new technologies, promote advanced designs and design methods, introduce new and more efficient production techniques, marketing and construction concepts, or pioneer new engineering services and management methods. Chartered Engineers are variously engaged in technical and commercial leadership and possess effective interpersonal skills.

The high-level concepts contained within the UKSPEC form a common pattern throughout many other frameworks and this provides the starting point for mapping and compliance between frameworks.

Discussion on the UKSPEC

The UKSPEC is, by design, a very high-level document, being as it is the benchmark for demonstrating competence. As it is such a high-level document, the descriptions for each of the generic competencies is also at a very high level. It is due to the high-level nature of the descriptions that it is impossible to be assessed directly against the UKSPEC as such, as each of the descriptions is open to different interpretations. Therefore, it is necessary to have a specialised interpretation of the UKSPEC for specific industries or disciplines that is, effectively, where the rest of the frameworks described in this chapter come in. Each of the following frameworks may be thought of as a specialised filter that may be applied to the generic UKSPEC to provide a bespoke interpretation of its requirements.

THE INCOSE COMPETENCIES FRAMEWORK

Background

INCOSE is an international industrial body that was set up to further the aims of systems engineering. It is not the role of this book to enter into the great 'what is a systems engineer' debate, but it is probably a good idea to provide a very brief overview of exactly what is meant by the terms 'systems engineering' and 'systems engineer'. The discipline of systems engineering is concerned with the interdisciplinary practices and principles that enable the realisation of successful systems. By the term 'system' here, we mean: physical systems, electronic systems, software systems, people systems, political systems, environmental systems, and so on and, indeed, any combination of these systems. The role of a systems engineer, therefore, is to enable the development of such systems. The role of a systems engineer is **not** to maintain PCs. Unfortunately, the term 'systems engineer' is shared by people who enable systems engineering and maintainers of PCs. Although both types are people essential in today's society, in the context of this book, we always mean the former, rather than the latter. INCOSE is concerned with the former, rather than the latter and if you are curious as to what makes a good systems engineer, then the INCOSE systems engineering competencies framework is a good place to start.

The INCOSE framework ontology

The focus of the framework is concerned with the concept of 'Systems Engineering Ability' which is described in Figure 2.2.

Figure 2.2 High-level view of the INCOSE competencies framework

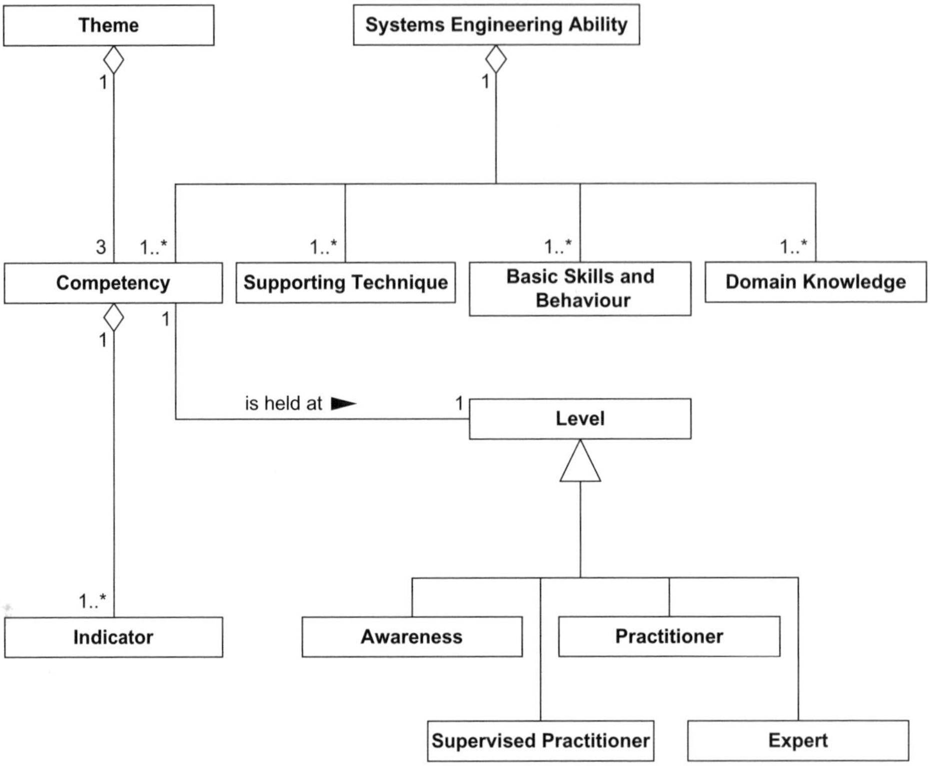

The INCOSE competencies framework has a concept of 'Systems engineering ability' that may be broken down into four main areas:

- Supporting Technique. A supporting technique is a specific technique that is used to support the main competencies, for example: failure analysis, decision analysis, the use of specific notations and languages, and so on. These techniques are very important but are not much value by themselves as it is when they are used to support and enable competencies that they start to add true benefits. These supporting techniques tend to be of a more technical nature and, therefore, easier to teach and measure. Due to the sheer number of these different techniques, the INCOSE framework does not go into any detail in this area, but simply provides a checklist to which one may want to refer when considering such techniques.

- Basic Skills and Behaviour. These represent the soft skills that are required in order to be a systems engineer, including skills such as: abstract thinking and communication (verbal/non-verbal, listening, writing, and so on). These softer skills tend to be less easy to teach or, indeed, to measure and can often rely on the objectivity of an assessor. Again, the INCOSE framework does not enter into much detail in this area and only provides a simple list of suggested areas that may be considered.

- Domain Knowledge. This knowledge is related directly to the domain in which the person is working. As systems engineering is a multi-disciplinary subject, it can cover, potentially, any domain. As the scope of 'any domain' is so wide, it is not covered in any detail in this framework.

- Competency. So far, the INCOSE framework has managed to sidestep all three of the areas covered, but the focus of the framework is very much on what is referred to as 'Competency', which refers to the core skills required for a systems engineer. These will be discussed in more detail in the remainder of this section.

The basic mapping between what is presented here and what exists in the UKSPEC seems relatively straightforward, but there is a potential ambiguity. The basic mapping is as follows:

- Both INCOSE concepts of 'Supporting Technique' and 'Basic Skill and Behaviour' map onto the UKSPEC concept of 'Skill'.

- The INCOSE concept of 'Domain Knowledge' maps onto the UKSPEC concept of 'Knowledge'.

- The INCOSE concept of 'Competency' maps onto the UKSPEC concept of 'Understanding'.

- The INCOSE concept of 'Systems Engineering Ability' maps onto the UKSPEC concept of 'Competency'.

The ambiguity should be quite clear from this mapping – the term 'Competency' has a different meaning in each of the frameworks. This is quite an important concept when considering competency assessment, so, when using the INCOSE framework, it is always worth having this ambiguity in mind.

The basic hierarchy of these competencies can be seen on the left-hand side of the diagram, which states that one or more 'Competency' is part of one of three types of 'Theme'. Each 'Competency' is made up of one or more 'Indicator(s)'. It is worth looking at each of these concepts in a little more detail.

The concept of a 'Theme' is really just a broad categorisation of competencies. The three themes that exist are:

- 'Systems Thinking', which is concerned with high-level, generic concepts associated with systems engineering. This theme covers the following competencies: 'Systems Concepts', 'Enterprise and Technical Environment' and 'Super System Capability Issues';

- 'Systems Engineering Management', which covers the aspects of management that are applicable to systems engineering. This theme covers the following competencies: 'Concurrent Engineering', 'Enterprise Integration', 'Integration of Specialisms', 'Life-cycle Process Definition' and 'Planning, Monitoring and Control';
- 'Holistic Life-cycle View', which covers the competencies that one may expect to see associated with the various best-practice systems engineering processes. This theme covers the following competencies: 'Determine and Manage Stakeholder Requirements', 'System Design' (that contains a further nine variations on systems design), 'Integration and Verification', 'Validation' and 'Transition to operation'.

Each of these competencies that have been identified in the previous list may be held at a particular level of competency. The INCOSE framework identifies four levels of competency:

1. 'Awareness'. The awareness level indicates that the person is able to understand basic concepts, to understand how the system fits into their enterprise and to be able to ask relevant questions associated with each competency. It may be that the person has no actual experience of the competency but does display some theoretical knowledge and understanding of it.

2. 'Supervised practitioner'. An individual who has competencies held at the supervised practitioner level will have some real experience of the competency. They will be able to display true understanding through the application of systems techniques and concepts as part of their work.

3. 'Practitioner'. An individual who has competencies held at the practitioner level will provide guidance and lead activity in this area. They will be able to supervise people at lower levels of competency and may very well lead teams or groups of people.

4. 'Expert'. The expert level represents those rare individuals who truly lead the field in a particular area. They are able to display their experience by defining best-practice, policy or process within an organisation or industry.

Each of the competencies that have been identified may be held at any of these four levels. At each of the levels and for each competency, there are a number of indicators defined, and it is these indicators that are actually assessed. Each indicator is a simple statement of what must be demonstrated to contribute towards meeting a competency. The indicator should be measurable in some accepted form.

Discussion

The INCOSE framework is the most immature of all the frameworks presented here. This is by no means intended to be a derogatory use of the term 'immature', but is simply intended to reflect the fact that the framework itself is relatively new and has not been through many iterations. Indeed, when compared to a framework like SFIA, the INCOSE framework is positively embryonic, but this is no bad thing. The INCOSE framework is simple and easy enough to understand and focuses on a specific aspect of competency, the systems engineering competencies, rather than trying to be a master of all disciplines, which is to be applauded.

With regard to the mechanics of the framework, there is a good example of a point that will be discussed later in the book, that of meeting lower levels. For example, at first glance, one would expect that if an individual attains the 'Practitioner' level for a competency, then surely they must also hold the 'Supervised Practitioner' level? This is logical and makes perfect sense, but is this the case here? Certainly there is nothing in the framework to state this explicitly and it will form a discussion point later in this book.

Also, because of the relatively few iterations that have been completed of the INCOSE framework, there are some areas, quite naturally, that are covered in more detail than others. For example, the 'System Design: Concept Generation' competency, at the 'Supervised Practitioner' level has single indicator defined. This means that a person will either pass or fail here and there is no room for argument. Take, on the other hand, the 'Determine and Manage Stakeholder Requirements' competency held at the same level – it has eight indicators defined, meaning that it may be possible to demonstrate seven out of eight indicators potentially to achieve a pass at this level. This can become quite a concern when trying to achieve consistency of results of an assessment. Returning to the point of the immaturity of the framework, however, these are all issues that can be sorted out quite simply in subsequent releases of the framework.

In terms of assessment of the INCOSE framework, there is a set of guidelines for assessment. However these are really a more detailed description of each of the indicators rather than an assessment mechanism as such. Also related to this is the Certified Systems Engineering Practitioner (CSEP) scheme (see CSEP) that has several levels of certification: entry level (Associate Systems Engineering Professional), foundation level (Certified Systems Engineering Professional) and senior level (Expert Systems Engineering Professional). There is also currently one extension to this which covers the USA Department of Defense Acquisition. In order to become certified, it is necessary to apply, pay a fee, sit an exam (at some levels) and attend an interview (at some levels). It should be borne in mind, however, that this is not a competency assessment as such but a certification, so the result will be a pass or fail, rather than a graded profile.

SFIA

Background
The SFIA is a framework used predominantly in the IT industry and which identifies the skills required to develop effective ISs and makes use of ICT.

The framework itself is owned, managed and configured by the SFIA Foundation, which is made up of the following members:

- the British Computer Society (BCS), the 'Chartered Institute for IT' (see BCS);

- E-skills UK, the sector skills council for business and information technology (see ESKILLS);

- the Institution for Engineering and Technology (IET), one of the world's largest professional societies (see IET);

- the Institute for Management of Information Systems (IMIS), an international professional body associated with IT management (see IMIS);

- the IT Service Management Forum (ITSMF), a truly independent worldwide forum for IT management professionals (see ITSMF).

The framework has an intended audience of:

- IT professionals and their managers. This includes anybody associated with IT, whether it is providing a product or service operating these IT systems. Notice here that it is assumed that IT managers have a technical background and actually understand what IT is. This is reflected in some of the other stakeholders who are specifically defined as having a non-technical background.

- Human resource managers. This includes anybody involved in recruitment, placement of people in different jobs, competency definition and assessment and so on. Notice that there is no specific requirement here for any particular technical or domain knowledge.

- Non-technical managers. These managers may be people who are involved with management but who do not have a technical or IT background. Of course, there will be a different skillset required for the different types of manager, so it is important that they can be differentiated.

- Internal staff-training personnel and people interested in CPD. It may be perceived here that there is an overlap with HR managers, which may very well be the case. However, there is a strong requirement for a CPD role that is not connected to HR in many organisations. It is increasingly common to find specific departments with their own drivers for competence and competency assessment that are part of a technical department, rather than being seen as remote and inside the HR department.

- People working in professional bodies. It may seem very obvious, but people who work in professional bodies have a strong requirement for understanding what competence is and how it can be measured. Bearing in mind that one of the main requirements for any professional body is providing a mechanism for CPD, then the definition and use of frameworks is a no-brainer.

- Lecturers, trainers and people involved with developing curricula for education. In order to demonstrate effective courses and training resources, it is essential that they meet the needs of the industry. By having a good understanding of the SFIA framework, it is possible to map the key course aspects to the framework, hence ensuring that the training satisfies the requirements of the framework.

- Government personnel. In order to achieve any sort of consistency across the public sector, it is crucial that the government, and its employees, share the same vision of what skills are needed by staff.

- People working in IT service organisations. It is not just the people providing the IT infrastructure and applications, but also the associated services that make up the IT industry as a whole. It is important, therefore, that all aspects of the IT industry can be represented by the framework.

With this in mind, it is now time to look at the key concepts and terminology that are used in the SFIA framework, by considering the SFIA ontology.

The SFIA ontology

The framework itself is made up of a two-dimensional matrix that is described in Figure 2.3.

Figure 2.3 SFIA framework ontology

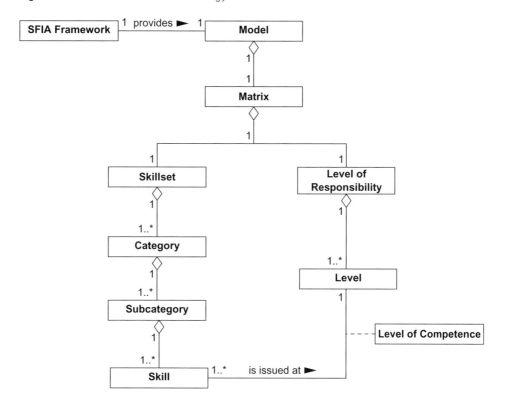

It can be seen here that the 'SFIA Framework' provides a 'Model' that is made up of a single 'Matrix'. This is made up of two main elements that are the 'Skillset' and the 'Level of Responsibility'. The 'Skillset' here refers to the broad categorisation of all IT skills that is made up of a number of 'Category(ies)'. Each 'Category' is made up of one or more 'Subcategory(ies)', each of which is made up of one or more 'Skill(s)'. This basic structural hierarchy provides the two levels of categorisation (excluding the highest level, 'Skillset' which encompasses everything) and the actual skills themselves, which are the elements that are actually assessed. Each skill has a four-letter abbreviation that provides a unique identifier.

The other dimension of the matrix is the 'Level of Responsibility' that is made up of one or more 'Level(s)'. In SFIA there are seven levels that exist and it is this level that relates to the actual skill that is being assessed. The level at which a particular skill is held is the 'Level of Competence' for an individual in that area. The categories that make up the skillset are:

- the 'Strategy and Planning' category, which is made up of: information strategy, advice and guidance, business/IS strategy and planning, and technical strategy and planning;
- the 'Development' category, which is made up of: systems development, human factors, and installation and integration;
- the 'Business change' category, which is made up of: business change management and relationship management.
- the 'Service provision' category, which is made up of: infrastructure, operation and user support;
- the 'Procurement and management support' category, which is made up of: supply management, quality and resource management;
- the 'Ancillary skills' category, which is made up of: education and training, and sales and marketing.

In terms of the levels, they are defined under the four attributes of: autonomy, influence, complexity and business skills. Each level has, basically, four main headings that are used to define each attribute and the combination of these four descriptions provides the overall description for the level. These levels may be broadly described as follows:

1. 'Follow'. A person with a skill held at level 1 is expected to be supervised most of the time and seek advice often. They are not expected to make any significant decisions, but will possess a basic knowledge of the skill.

2. 'Assist'. A person with a skill held at level 2 is expected to work under minor supervision and to only seek advice where necessary. They are expected to begin to use their judgement in making minor decisions.

3. 'Apply'. A person with a skill held at level 3 is expected to work under general supervision and will be able to make a decision as to when and where advice should be sought.

4. 'Enable'. A person with a skill held at level 4 will work only under general direction and will have a clear set of responsibilities. They will also plan their own work and follow processes.

5. 'Ensure, advise'. A person with a skill held at level 5 will work under a very broad direction but will hold full responsibility and accountability in a specific area of work. They will also set their own work goals, plans and objectives and delegate assignments.

6. 'Initiate, influence'. A person with a skill held at level 6 will have defined responsibility and accountability for a significant area of work. They are also accountable for decisions made by themselves and others below them.

7. 'Set strategy'. A person with a skill held at level 7 will have significant responsibility and authority and will be involved in defining policy. They will also be accountable for the decisions of any people working as their subordinates.

These levels can be used as a basis for mapping onto an organisation's specific framework where necessary or may be used as stand-alone definitions.

Discussion

One of the immediate observations that strikes many people is the sheer size of the SFIA framework. There are almost 80 skills held at seven levels, which is visualised via a large chart. At first, this can be quite intimidating, but it should be noted that it is the complexity of an entity rather than its size that makes something difficult to understand and, despite its size, SFIA is well structured and defined and deceptively easy to follow.

There are seven levels of responsibility here – most other frameworks only have four or five. This is not a problem and, indeed, it is easier to map to fewer levels than it is to map to more levels (i.e. mapping from seven levels to four is less complex than mapping four levels to seven). The sheer number of levels can put some people off the framework.

The skills themselves and the categorisations shown are really for illustration only. It is made quite clear that it is the actual skills themselves that are important rather than how they are categorised. Indeed, people are encouraged to define their own structure of classification and not just to use SFIA in an off-the-shelf manner.

Like many of these frameworks, the emphasis is largely focused on the technical skills rather than the soft or human skills that may be required for a person. This is a problem that is common to many of the frameworks, but it should be borne in mind that a boundary must be put onto a framework somewhere and this boundary is quite clear in SFIA.

With the number of skills that are identified here, there are some surprising omissions from the technical areas described. One specific area that may be a cause for concern is the area of requirements engineering that is not really addressed in the framework.

The SFIA framework is very mature and has a large and formal process of continuous improvement, dedicated conferences and a massive uptake of its use in the IT industry. In terms of assessment, individuals can become SFIA-accredited consultants; this involves an assessment fee and attending a course to become a listed consultant. This only means that the assessed person is recognised as being able to give advice on SFIA skill areas, so it is not an assessment mechanism as such.

THE ASSOCIATION OF PROJECT MANAGEMENT (APM)

Background

The APM is the largest independent professional body for management in Europe, whose mission is to 'develop and promote the professional disciplines of project and programme management for the public benefit'.

The knowledge and experience of its extensive membership is captured in the 'Body of Knowledge' that forms the cornerstone of competency assessment and demonstration for project and programme managers. The target audience for the APM is project and programme managers, although it can be and is used extensively by other roles and organisations.

The APM ontology

The concept of APM competency in the APM relies on two main elements – the 'Framework' and the 'Body of Knowledge' which can be seen in the following diagram.

Figure 2.4 The APM framework ontology

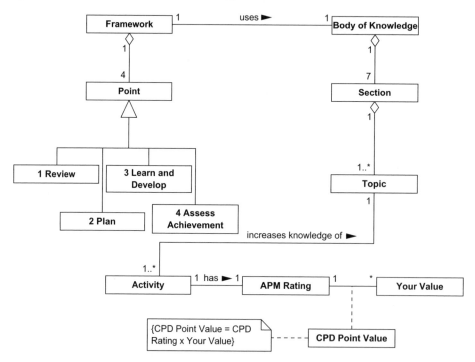

Figure 2.4 shows the APM ontology and it can be seen that the 'Framework' uses the 'Body of Knowledge'. The 'Framework' is made up of four 'Points', each of which has a number of questions or pieces of advice associated with it that the person must address. These are described as follows:

- '1 Review' refers to an individual's ability to look at their own abilities and ask four questions: 'what skills do I have?', 'what have I achieved?', 'what have I learned?' and 'how appropriate are my skills to my current work situation?' The answers to these questions are recorded in the individual's personal record. It is suggested that an initial self-assessment is used to generate these answers.

- '2 Plan' refers to an individual's ability to plan how to get from where they are to where the want to be. The questions that need to be answered are: 'what gaps are there in my current knowledge and skills?', 'what can I do to fill these gaps?', 'where do I want to be in five years time?' and 'what do I need to do to achieve this and who can help me?' The answers to these questions are recorded in the individual's personal development plan, where their objectives are listed in relation to these questions.

- '3 Learn and Develop' refers to an individual's ability to execute this plan and to capture any relevant information. The advice that is offered here is: 'keep a record of everything you have achieved', 'we are all different, you may learn in a different way to your colleagues', 'there will be opportunities to learn and develop that aren't in your original plan'. Rather than questions, these are pieces of advice that should be followed at all times. In fairness, they are good, solid, common-sense ideas that should be reflected in all aspects of CPD, not just limited to management frameworks.

- '4 Assess Achievement' refers to an individual's ability to understand what has been achieved and how it helps. The questions that must be answered are: 'what have I learnt?', 'how does this help me now?', 'how might it help me in the future?' and 'do I need anything to enhance this learning?' The answers to these questions are recorded in the individual's development record, which can then be used as a basis for generating CVs, used in interviews, or wherever else is deemed appropriate.

Each of these points is executed as part of an ongoing cycle and in the order shown above. This may be thought of as being like a continuous professional development iteration that is executed time and time again throughout the life cycle of an individual's career.

The basis of all the questions that are asked here is that a set of skills must be identified by the individual, and this is where the 'Body of Knowledge' comes in. The 'Body of Knowledge' itself is made up of seven 'Section(s)' each of which is made up of one or more 'Topic(s)'. These sections and their associated topics may be further described as follows (Note, these sections and topics are omitted from the diagram for the sake of clarity. For a full description of these sections and topics, see SFIA.):

- The '1 – Project management in context' section is made up of the following topics: '1.1 Project management', '1.2 Programme management', '1.3 Portfolio management', '1.4 Project context', '1.5 Project sponsorship' and '1.6 Project office'.

- The '2 – Planning the strategy' section is made up of the following topics: '2.1 Project success and benefits management', '2.2 Stakeholder management', '2.3 Value management', '2.4 Project management plan', '2.5 Project risk management', '2.6 Project quality management' and '2.7 Health, safety and environmental management'.

- The '3 – Executing the strategy' section is made up of the following topics: '3.1 Scope management', '3.2 Scheduling', '3.3 Resource management', '3.4 Budgeting and cost management', '3.5 Change control', '3.6 Earned value management', '3.7 Information management', ' 3.8 Issue management'.

- The '4 – Techniques' section is made up of the following topics: '4.1 Requirements management', '4.2 Development', '4.3 Estimating', '4.4 Technology management', '4.5 Value engineering', '4.6 Modelling and testing' and '4.7 Configuration management'.

- The '5 – Business and commercial' section is made up of the following topics: '5.1 Business case', '5.2 Marketing and sales', '5.3 Project financing and funding', '5.4 Procurement' and '5.5 Legal awareness'.

- The '6 – Organisation and governance' section is made up of the following topics: '6.1 Project life cycles', '6.2 Concept', '6.3 Definition', '6.4 Implementation', '6.5 Handover and closeout', '6.6 Project reviews', '6.7 Organisation structure', '6.8 Organisational roles', '6.9 Methods and procedures' and '6.10 Governance of project management'.

- The '7 – People and the profession' section is made up of the following topics: '7.1 Communication', '7.2 Teamwork', '7.3 Leadership', '7.4 Conflict management', '7.5 Negotiation', '7.6 Human resources management', '7.7 Behavioural characteristics', '7.8 Learning and development', '7.9 Professionalism and ethics'.

Each of these topics will have a number of activities associated with it that help to increase the knowledge of a particular topic. These activities include: work-based on-the-job training, informal CPD, formal events and qualifications (not shown on the diagram for the sake of clarity). Each of these activities is given an 'APM Rating' which may be 1, 2, 3, or 5 (no '4') that provides a weighting for making the calculation to derive the 'CPD points value'. The individual then decides how valuable the information that has been learned is, by defining the 'Your Value' on a scale of 2 to 10 where '2' is considered to be of 'little value' and '10' is considered to be of 'high value'. These two values – the 'APM Rating' and the 'Your Value' – are then multiplied to provide the 'CPD Points Value', which may then be used to provide evidence of competency.

Discussion

The APM framework is particularly interesting as it relies, to quite a large extent, on continuous self-assessment. As part of this assessment, the individual can actually put values onto how valuable the new skills are and use these to show potential employers, professional bodies (for professional qualifications, such as Chartered Project Manager) and for internal company assessments.

It is important when applying these techniques in the APM framework that they are based on realistic estimates of how valuable things are for an individual. Part of the danger of such a numbered scheme is that it is open to abuse. It would be hoped that within a professional discipline, this would not occur, but there is always a need for validating assessments and claims made based on self-assessments.

There may be nothing sinister about somebody over-estimating their own values because, as discussed previously in this book, incompetent people tend to over-estimate their own competence.

Accreditation

There is a formal accreditation scheme in place that allows people to be trained and assessed to a number of levels. These are:

1. 'APM introductory certificate in project management', which is an entry-level qualification that covers the basics of project management and requires the candidate to sit an exam;

2. 'APM practitioner qualification', which assesses an individual to demonstrate their practical experience in assisting in the management of projects, and requires the candidate to sit an exam;

3. 'APM certified project manager', which is a formal three-stage process leading to full formal recognition as a certified project manager. This level is really what the focus of this book is about – full competency assessment, rather than sitting an exam and gaining a qualification.

In order to gain these qualifications, it is essential that any training provided is recognised by the APM under their 'accredited provider' scheme.

THE ASSOCIATION OF PROPOSAL MANAGEMENT PROFESSIONALS

Background

The APMP is the professional body that defines and supports best practice in the areas of bids, proposals and business acquisition. The APMP has defined a set of competencies that are required in order to become a proposal management professional.

The APMP ontology

The APMP ontology describes a multi-level hierarchy that can be seen in Figure 2.5.

It can be seen from Figure 2.5 that the 'APMP Framework' is made up of six 'Syllabus Group(s)', each of which is made up of one or more 'Syllabus Area(s)', each of which is made up of one or more 'Competence(s)'. The syllabus groups and their associated syllabus areas are described as follows:

1. The 'Information Research and Management' syllabus group is made up of the following syllabus areas: 'Information Gathering' and 'Knowledge Management'.

2. The 'Planning' syllabus group is made up of the following single syllabus area: 'Schedule Development'.

3. The 'Development' syllabus group is made up of the following syllabus areas: 'Opportunity Qualification', 'Winning Price Development', 'Teaming Identification', 'Proposal Strategy Development', 'Executive Summary Development', 'Storyboard Development', 'Requirements Identification', 'Compliance Checklist Development' and 'Outline Development'.

4. The 'Management' syllabus group is made up of the following syllabus areas: 'Storyboard Review Management', 'Kick-off Meeting Management', 'Review Management', 'Proposal Risk Management', Proposal Progress reporting', 'Final Document Review Management', 'Production Management', 'Lessons Learnt Analysis and Management' and 'Proposal Process Management'.

5. The 'Sales Orientation' syllabus group is made up of the following syllabus areas: 'Customer Interface Management', 'Capture Plan Development', 'Winning Strategy Development', 'Negotiation Planning' and 'Sales Participation'.

Figure 2.5 The APMP ontology

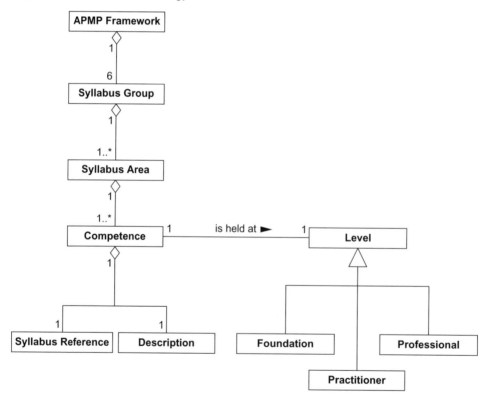

6. The 'Behaviour and Attitude' syllabus group is made up of the following syllabus areas: 'Communication and Persuasiveness', 'Quality Orientation', 'Building Strategic Relationships and a Successful Team' and 'Decision Making and Delegating Responsibility'.

Each of these syllabus areas has a number of competencies defined in a simple table format with a 'Syllabus Reference' and 'Description'. Each of these competencies may be held at one of three 'Level(s)', as follows:

1. The APMP 'Foundation' level indicates that an individual can act as part of a proposal or bid team. They will be able to follow processes and use tools as well as understanding the basic principles and approaches to work.

2. The APMP 'Practitioner' level indicates that an individual can run and manage a bid or proposal within an organisation. This includes being able to tailor any approach to a specific project, for instance to address the needs and problems of a customer response.

3. The APMP 'Professional' level indicates that an individual can drive the continuous improvement of the proposal or bid management processes within an organisation.

The APMP framework also includes a simple process that may be followed to achieve professional accreditation.

Discussion
The APMP is one of the lesser-known, but arguably more mature organisations. It holds a number of high-quality events, has an extensive and impressive membership (and list of sponsors) and has developed a rigid process for accreditation. This process is very good, but some argue that putting a definitive requirement on the number of years' experience required can be off-putting to some people, particularly high-flyers who consider themselves to be on a fast-track to accreditation.

The APMP also fills a gap that is not covered in any detail by any of the other frameworks mentioned here. The whole area of proposal management is one that is often overlooked but is, arguably, one of the most important aspects of the business to get right. After all, if an organisation does not win any bids, then it will have a severely restricted income.

Accreditation
The APMP specifies a formal process of examination, self-assessment and interview that allows a candidate to pass through the three levels of competence to full, recognised professional status. The actual process and its requirements are summarised very neatly in Table 2.1, taken from the APMP website (see APMP).

Table 2.1 Summary of accreditation requirements for the APMP

	Foundation	**Practitioner**	**Professional**
Referee required	Yes	Yes	Yes
Number of years prior experience required	1	3	7
Tests	Basic knowledge of best practice	Application of best practice	Advocacy of best practice
Type of assessment required	Multiple choice examination	Online self-assessment	Reference, presentation and interview
Continuing education unit required per two-year period	20	40	40

The APMP also offers two levels of membership, which are 'Member' and 'Fellow', each of which comes with its own set of designations.

CHOOSING BETWEEN FRAMEWORKS

Introduction

When it comes to choosing between frameworks, then the scope of each and their intended audience becomes very important. This can lead to problems, however, as it is very rare that a single person will have their entire skillset chosen by a single framework. For example, imagine an individual who works in the proposal management department of an organisation and spends their working life preparing proposals. The obvious choice for this candidate is the APMP framework that is geared solely towards this type of person. However, now consider that this person works in the systems engineering industry, then surely the INCOSE framework would also be of interest to them. There is a need, therefore, to be able to map between these frameworks and to provide a mechanism to mix and match skills from different sources to generate a more complete scope (assessment input) and, hence, profile (assessment output).

One way to address this is to look for a common reference that can be used as a starting point for mapping between the various competency frameworks. In the frameworks that have been considered in this book, there is a convenient framework onto which all of the others map that provides a ready-made starting point for this exercise. The UKSPEC forms the benchmark for professional recognition for all of the frameworks here and is, therefore, the ideal candidate for this mapping.

Mappings

In order to map between the competency frameworks, therefore, it is necessary to map each one individually onto the UKSPEC and this can then be used as an interface to map between the frameworks. For the purposes of this book, a full mapping is not feasible in terms of the number of pages (and trees) that would be required to print this information. Therefore, a partial mapping will be shown between some of UKSPEC and some of three of the frameworks. The scope of this mapping exercise will be limited to:

- One set of generic competencies – 'A: education, training and experience'. These are the first ones in the framework and are chosen for no other reason than convenience.

- The first 10 skills or competencies from each of the chosen frameworks. These were, again, chosen as the first ones in the framework and the number of 10 was arrived at purely to keep the tables readable.

- The frameworks considered, which will be: SFIA, APM and the INCOSE competencies framework. Again, these were chosen arbitrarily and with a firm eye on the number of pages that would be required to reprint any more mappings.

With this scope in mind, the mappings are as shown in the following Tables 2.2, 2.3 and 2.4.

Table 2.2 shows the partial mapping between SFIA and the UKSPEC. Notice how, with this scope, there is only a single mapping shown. This is not necessarily a poor reflection on SFIA but, rather, shows where the focus of the two frameworks overlaps.

Table 2.3 shows the partial mapping between the APM and the UKSPEC. Notice that there are more mappings here compared to those shown in the SFIA table but, again, this does not necessarily reflect the frameworks as a whole, just the scopes that were chosen here.

Table 2.4 shows the mapping between the INCOSE competencies framework and the UKSPEC. Again, there are a number of mappings here, but nowhere near a complete set.

Discussion

In order to demonstrate how these tables may be used in reality, imagine that a simple scope (input for an assessment) is set to being the UKSPEC generic competencies shown here (the 'A' competencies shown on the vertical axis on the tables). In order to demonstrate each generic competency, we will be looking for a specific interpretation of that competency in a source framework, hence the use of the tables.

Tables 2.2, 2.3 and 2.4 each provide a different set of mappings. One immediate thing that stands out is where there is a lack of mappings. This can lead to a number of possible conclusions:

Table 2.2 Partial mapping between SFIA and UKSPEC

	ACMG – Account Management	ANAL – Business Analysis	ARCH – Systems Architecture	ASMG – Asset Management	ASUP – Application Support	AVMT – Availability Management	BENM – Benefits Management	BPRE – Business Process Improvement	BPTS – Business Process Testing	BURM – Business Risk Management
A1.1: Awareness of Personal Knowledge and Skills										
A1.2: Enhancement of Technical Skills										
A1.3: Enhancement of Knowledge										
A2.1: Stakeholder Requirements										
A2.2: Marketing Strategy										
A2.3: Opportunity Exploitation										
A2.4: Application Promotion										
A2.5: IPR Awareness										
A2.6: Continuous Improvement								X		

- There is no mapping, because there is an omission from the source framework. This is possible but not very likely, bearing in mind the maturity of the frameworks and the amount of work and effort that has gone into producing them.

- There is no mapping, because the mapping is outside the scope of the source framework. This is possible and far more likely. As was discussed previously, each framework has a boundary that falls in a different place and it is, therefore, natural that there will be areas, in many cases large areas, where the mapping will not exist. This is particularly true when one bears in mind that the UKSPEC applies to the whole of engineering and science, whereas each framework only represents a subset of this.

- There is no mapping because there is some misunderstanding about what exactly is meant in one or more of the source frameworks. This is also possible and, unfortunately, in some cases, all too true. This may be because the framework is poorly written, but, in most cases, this will be because the person reading the framework does not hold an appropriate level of competence to understand matters fully.

The next aspect of the mappings to consider is where mappings exist for more than one framework. For example, consider the mapping between: Table 2.3: 'A2.2: Marketing Strategy' – 'CC01 – Project Sponsorship', and Table 2.4: 'A2.2: Marketing Strategy' – 'Enterprise Integration'. The fact that there is a common mapping between the two tables means that there is some relationship between

Table 2.3 Partial mapping between APM and UKSPEC

	BC01 – Communication	BC02 – Teamwork	BC03 – Leadership	BC04 – Conflict Management	BC05 – Negotiation	BC06 – Human Resource Management	BC07 – Behavioural Characteristics	BC08 – Learning and Development	BC09 – Professionalism and Ethics	CC01 – Project Sponsorship
A1.1: Awareness of Personal Knowledge and Skills							X	X		
A1.2: Enhancement of Technical Skills								X		
A1.3: Enhancement of Knowledge								X		
A2.1: Stakeholder Requirements										
A2.2: Marketing Strategy										X
A2.3: Opportunity Exploitation										
A2.4: Application Promotion										
A2.5: IPR Awareness										
A2.6: Continuous Improvement								X		

Table 2.4 Partial mapping between the INCOSE competencies framework and UKSPEC

	Architectural Design	Concept Generation	Concurrent Engineering	Design For ...	Determining And Manage Stakeholder Requirements	Enterprise and Technology Environment	Enterprise Integration	Functional analysis	Holistic Life-cycle View	Integration of Specialisms
A1.1: Awareness of Personal Knowledge and Skills										
A1.2: Enhancement of Technical Skills										
A1.3: Enhancement of Knowledge										
A2.1: Stakeholder Requirements					X					
A2.2: Marketing Strategy							X			
A2.3: Opportunity Exploitation						X				
A2.4: Application Promotion										
A2.5: IPR Awareness						X				
A2.6: Continuous Improvement										

the mappings, but does not in any way mean that the two represent the same thing. To emphasise this, by cross-correlating between these two tables, it is possible to deduce that:

1. 'CC01 – Project Sponsorship' from APM and 'Enterprise Integration' from INCOSE are related;

2. 'CC01 – Project Sponsorship' from APM and 'Enterprise Integration' from INCOSE are not necessarily the same thing.

These mappings will only ever be able to show up **potential** similarities by identifying relationships through the mappings. In order to understand wherever these two skills represent the same thing, then it is essential that a competent person makes a judgement call as to whether they are the same and, if they are not, why not and how they do relate.

There are two conclusions that can be made based on this mapping:

1. If the skills are not the same, then which one is more appropriate for the scope that we are assessing against? It may be that both are required, but it is important that an informed decision is made.

2. If the skills are the same, then we can assume that we can demonstrate meeting both competencies at once, hence saving time and effort.

There are clearly many gaps in the mapping, as seen from these tables, but it has to be borne in mind that this is a very incomplete set of mappings and there are many more columns in the actual tables that do provide a lot more coverage of the UKSPEC generic competencies.

CONCLUSIONS

This chapter has introduced a number of competency frameworks that are used in a number of different industries. Each of these frameworks has a different scope, purpose and audience. Each of these frameworks is also recognised in its own particular field of interest and can be used, to different extents, as part of continuous professional development.

No single framework will provide all relevant skills for a single person, therefore, in many cases, it may be desirable to choose different skills from different frameworks and to map them together. An example of this was shown using the UKSPEC but, in reality, any source framework could be used or, indeed, a generic framework could be generated to perform this mapping – in fact, this is exactly what is done in the next chapter, where frameworks are mapped onto a generic framework to be used as a basis for competency assessment.

Now that frameworks have been introduced and discussed, it is time to look at how the information gathered from each framework can be used to generate a set of requirements that is needed to perform assessments against any framework.

REFERENCES

Framework information sources
APM www.apm.org.uk/ (Accessed February 2011). The APM website contains a lot of high-level information about the framework and how to go about accreditation. There are overviews of the Body of Knowledge available for free download, but the full information set is only available to purchase.

APMP www.apmp.org/ (Accessed February 2011). The APMP website contains a lot of high-level information about the framework and how to go about accreditation. There are overviews of the framework available for free download, but the full information set is only available to purchase.

INCOSE www.incose.org/ProductsPubs/products/competenciesframework.aspx (Accessed February 2011). The INCOSE website contains information on all aspects of systems engineering and a high-level description of the framework. In order to download the framework, it is necessary to be a member of INCOSE or contact them directly.

SFIA www.sfia.org.uk/ (Accessed February 2011). This is the website for the SFIA Foundation and contains a colossal amount of information about SFIA. This includes an excellent download section with the specifications, summary booklets and a very useful, if somewhat large, wall chart.

UKSPEC www.engc.org.uk/professional-qualifications/standards/uk-spec (Accessed February 2011). This is the website for the Engineering Council and provides a wealth of information on CPD generally and free downloads of the UKSPEC documentation set.

Other organisations

BCS www.bcs.org/ (Accessed February 2011). The BCS – the Chartered Institute for IT (formerly known as the British Computer Society)

CSEP www.incose.org/educationcareers/certification/ (Accessed February 2011). The Certified Systems Engineering Professional scheme.

ESKILLS www.e-skills.com/ (Accessed February 2011). The eSkills Council

IET www.theiet.org/ (Accessed February 2011). The Institution of Engineering and Technology

IMIS www.imis.org.uk/ (Accessed February 2011). The Institute for Management of Information Systems

ITSMF www.itsmf.co.uk/ (Accessed February 2011). The IT Service Management Forum

Useful books

Holt, J. (2009) *A pragmatic guide to business process modelling,* second edition. BCS, the Chartered Institute for IT, Swindon.

3 REQUIREMENTS FOR COMPETENCY ASSESSMENT

I can talk these words that will sound so sweet. They will even make your little heart skip a beat. Heal the sick, raise the dead. Make the little girls talk outta their heads. I'm the one
Seventh Son, Johnny Rivers

INTRODUCTION

So far, a broad introduction of competence and competency assessment has been presented and discussed along with some of the more widely recognised competency frameworks. However, if anything, identifying or producing the framework is only part of the battle, as the issue of assessment must also be addressed.

REQUIREMENTS FOR AN ASSESSMENT PROCESS

When assessing competence, it is essential that we have a well-understood and well-defined approach. In the business or industrial world, an essential part of any approach is a well-defined process. Therefore, in order to carry out effective and efficient assessments, it is essential that we have a process in place.

When thinking about any process for assessment, there are a number of requirements that exist for the process:

- The process must be repeatable. It is essential that any process that is put in place is repeatable. By this, we mean that the process can be carried out more than once in exactly the same way from assessment to assessment. There are three main reasons for this, which are trending personal assessments, comparing multiple assessments and to allow assessors to be trained effectively. When an individual has an assessment carried out, then it goes without saying that the results should be useful. These results become even more useful, however, when they can be trended over time. For example, it may be desirable to have a competency assessment carried out every year. Once this has been done more than once, it is possible to then see the competency trend, or the evolution of competency over time. A competency assessment only provides a single snapshot view of competency and cannot show how it changes over time. This evolution of competency is very powerful as it can demonstrate how a person's skills and abilities have changed over time. The second reason why a repeatable process is necessary is because it is also desirable to compare the assessment results of more than one person. For example, if two people were applying for the same job or promotion, then it may be decided that a competency assessment would be an important input to this decision. In such a situation, then it is clear that the results of two assessments cannot be compared unless they have followed the same process for the assessment itself. The third reason concerns the assessors themselves.

Assessors must be competent in their own right (discussed later in this chapter) and part of this competence must be familiarity with the process itself. If the process is different for every assessment, then it becomes very difficult, if not impossible, to ensure that the assessors possess the necessary levels of knowledge and rigour required by the assessment.

- The process must have transferable results. When someone has been assessed within a particular organisation, then the results will be recognised within that organisation. But what happens when that person applies for a job in another company – are the same results still recognised? One of the most desirable features for competency assessments is true transferability of results, as the same competency framework can be interpreted in different ways by different assessors. Whether the results of assessments can ever truly be universally transferable is a question that can never be answered fully in the positive, but it is argued here that it is simply impossible even to begin to consider transferable results without a common process. Therefore, within certain communities, and given the appropriate training and experience, transferable results can certainly be achieved.

- The process must be measurable. The old adage goes that if something can't be measured, then it cannot be managed, and competency assessment is no exception. When considering competency assessment, it is absolutely crucial that the results can be measured. With any type of assessment, the output will be limited in its utility, depending on what you do with the results. If the results are measurable, then it becomes possible for all sorts of statistical and trend analyses to be performed. Indeed, the next chapter will discuss the processes that can be used after an assessment has taken place and these are where the value of the assessment is truly realised.

- The process must be based on best practice. Countless hours of work go into assessments of all different types and there is, therefore, an awful lot of work that has already been carried out in this area, albeit in different application domains. It is possible, therefore, to learn from these other areas and to reuse the assessment knowledge. Also, when processes are based on best practice, such as standards and published approaches, it inspires more confidence in the whole process.

- The process must be tailorable. As with any best-practice approach, the process itself will, by its very nature, be generic and therefore not specific enough for most people. Any process, therefore, must be tailorable so that it can be made to fit the requirements of a particular organisation. All best-practice processes should be treated as 'guidance only' and should be tailored for your business. Of course, the more tailored a process becomes, then the further away from the source it becomes, which in itself brings its own problems. The greatest risk with tailoring a process too much is that the process loses all recognition with the original and, therefore, will not meet the other requirements for a process in this list.

When considering a process for assessment, it is important that it is judged based on these requirements, so that an informed decision can be made as the suitability of the process for the business at hand.

INTRODUCING THE UNIVERSAL COMPETENCY ASSESSMENT MODEL (UCAM)

The process that is proposed in this book is known as the Universal Competency Assessment Model (UCAM). The idea of UCAM is to provide a set of generic core processes that can be used as a basis for competency assessment in any business, in any domain and using any competency framework. The essence of UCAM is four core processes that form the heart of any assessment. These processes will provide an assessment result, but will need to be augmented by other bespoke processes to make the results truly useful. The UCAM processes are described in detail in the next chapter, but UCAM addresses the five requirements of a competency assessment process in the following ways:

- Repeatable. By having a rigorously defined process, it is possible to have a repeatable process. The UCAM process is defined using the 'seven-views' approach to process definition which, when applied and executed correctly, ensures that the process will be repeatable.

- Transferable results. The output to any assessment using UCAM can be compared to and recognised by any other assessment using UCAM. The key here is that the process that has been used to carry out the assessment is the same (see UCAM) and that the format of the results themselves are the same. Therefore, given that the approach followed is the same and the results look the same, then the results are potentially transferable. There is another criterion here, as the assessors who carry out the assessments must themselves be competent.

- Measurable. The output of the UCAM assessments all take the same format and have a set of well-defined attributes that can be used for more formal measurements, such as statistical and trend analyses.

- Based on best practice. The process behind UCAM is based on best-practice capability assessment processes, such as CMMI (see CMMI) and SPICE (see SPICE). The theory behind this is that if both capability and competence represent ability at different levels (capability at a business level and competence at a personal level) then the underlying processes must share some common features. As thousands of man-years of effort have been put into creating a number of well-defined and now mature processes for capability assessment, it seems obvious to make use of this wealth of knowledge and experience when defining UCAM.

- Tailorable. The UCAM processes are designed to be generic and tailorable. Examples of this are provided in Chapter 5, where some tailored examples of UCAM are discussed.

Of course, there will be other approaches to competency assessment rather than the one proposed here, but these basic requirements remain the same for any approach.

SELF-ASSESSMENT VERSUS THIRD-PARTY ASSESSMENT

When applying competency assessment, it is important to consider how it will be performed in a practical context. There are two main ways in which competency can be applied: self-assessment or third-party assessment.

Self-assessment is concerned with an individual carrying out the competency assessment on themselves, whereas third-party assessment has the assessment carried out by someone other than the individual. There are many pros and cons associated with each approach and this will be discussed by considering a number of issues.

The first issue is that of rigour. One of the biggest problems with self-assessment is that people who are less competent tend to have a higher opinion of themselves than people who know what they are doing – discussed in Chapter 1. To a certain extent, this can be addressed by having a well-defined process in place that can be used for both self-assessment and third-party assessment, but there is still the element of trust involved in the individual. It is always possible that an unscrupulous individual will either fake their own results or exaggerate their own claims to competence. With third-party assessment, the rigour is more assured than with self-assessment as the element of an individual being able to exaggerate their own abilities is removed. Of course, what this actually comes down to is the competence of the individual to carry out the assessment and, theoretically, if an individual was competent to perform competency assessments, then the result should be the same. However, it is unreasonable to expect every person to be fully trained and qualified to assess competency.

The second issues are ones of time and cost. At the end of the day, competency assessments take a not insignificant amount of time and resource. Some of the time and effort estimates for assessments will be discussed in the next chapter, but even for a simple assessment of, for example, six competencies at three levels, the estimate is in the region of two assessors for three hours to carry out an assessment. This may not seem like much for a single assessment, but consider the situation for carrying out 20, 50 or even 100 assessments. The numbers now seem to look quite daunting. Clearly, self-assessment comes into its own for multiple assessments as it is not really feasible to carry out large numbers of third-party assessments without incurring massive expenses. Therefore, when it comes to time and cost, then self-assessment is clearly the way forward.

The next issue is that of training the assessor. This has been touched on previously, but it really must be stressed that the competence of the assessor is key to successful assessments. In an ideal world, all people who would perform self-assessments should be trained to perform them effectively, but the issues of time and cost arise again. Clearly, it would cost a lot less to train up a few people for third-party assessment, or even to rely on third-party assessment from another organisation, hence incurring no training costs. Again, however, the issues of time and cost for these assessments must be borne in mind.

A more practical approach to assessing large numbers of people is a combination of self-assessment and third-party assessment. For example, consider the situation where 100 people need to be assessed. One pragmatic approach would be to get everyone to carry out a self-assessment and then to take a small sample, say 10, to be assessed by a third party. In this way, the people who do the self-assessments would always know that there is a chance that they will be selected to be fully assessed by a third party, which should keep people's exaggerations down to a minimum. In terms of training, it is feasible to provide a reduced, high-level training scheme for self-assessment in the form or process guides and seminars that can be applied to large numbers of people and provide them with just enough knowledge to carry out self-assessments. Of course, this should not be confused with having people who can carry out third-party assessments.

BEST PRACTICE

Common elements of competency frameworks
When looking at the competency frameworks that were introduced in Chapter 2, there are some striking similarities between some of the frameworks. If more than one framework have the same concepts within them, then it makes sense that this may be a 'good thing' that should be present in any framework. In this way, it is possible to abstract out a 'best set' of features for a framework. This approach of modelling and then abstracting common elements can be applied not only to the frameworks themselves, but also to the process of assessment itself. This approach has been applied and the information obtained has resulted in the development of a 'competency assessment meta-model' that forms the heart of the Universal Competency Assessment Model.

The competency assessment meta-model
The competency assessment meta-model captures the elements common to all competency frameworks in a model that forms the basis of the UCAM and that defines a common vocabulary that can be used when working with multiple frameworks. This abstracted common meta-model has four main elements, which will be discussed in turn: framework definition, framework population, assessment set-up and assessment.

Framework definition
The first element of the meta-model is concerned with framework definition. The idea is to come up with a common set of features that can then be mapped back to each of the frameworks that was discussed in Chapter 2. The framework definition element needs to be defined **once per framework** only. The only other time that this may need to be revisited is if the source framework changes and, in reality, this should be a small step unless the source framework changes significantly. The framework definition element of the meta-model is shown in the following diagram.

Figure 3.1 shows that the heart of framework definition is the concept of a 'Competency'. Each 'Competency' has a number of attributes that are:

- 'Description', a simple text description of the competency itself. This should be concise, to the point and not be overly verbose;

- 'Reason', the rationale behind why the competency is needed in the first place. This is very important as it provides a justification for why the competency is in the framework, so may include information such as which stakeholder roles require the competency;

- 'Title', the official name of the competency. This may also include, or be augmented by, a unique identifier that can be used both to reference and summarise the competency.

Figure 3.1 The 'framework definition' element of the meta-model

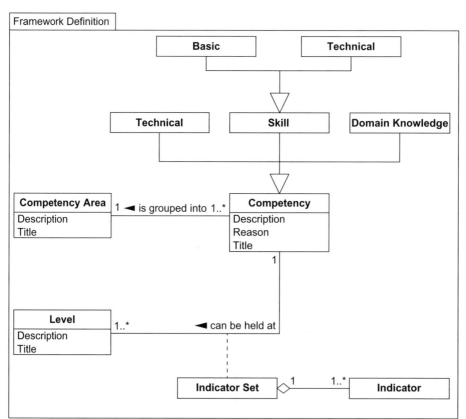

These competencies are classified into a simple competency taxonomy that contains the following types:

- 'Technical' competencies. These will form the heart of most frameworks as the frameworks tend to be focused on the technical side of things. These competencies will tend to map very well onto best-practice processes, whether they are in-house processes or ones that are derived from a standard. For example, the INCOSE competencies framework maps back very well to 'ISO 15288 – systems engineering life-cycle processes' (see ISO15288 2003), APM maps very well onto 'Prince II – projects in a controlled environment' (see PRINCE II 2009), and so on.

- 'Skill' competencies. These are further divided into 'Basic' and 'Technical'. The 'Basic' competencies here refer to some of the critical and abstract thinking skills, as well as communication skills, writing, presenting, and so on. The 'Technical' competencies will focus on individual techniques that may be applied to solve particular problems. Generically, these may include methodologies and techniques and may even be extended to include the use of specific tools.

- 'Domain Knowledge' competencies. These are the skills that are generally not included in the generic frameworks that have been discussed previously, as they will be specific to particular industries.

All of these competencies are grouped into a generic 'Competency Area'. This mechanism allows a hierarchy of competencies to be defined and keeps the whole framework more manageable and understandable. The competency areas are further described by a 'Description' and 'Title'. Each competency is held at a particular 'Level' via an 'Indicator Set'. It is the 'Indicator Set' (made up of one or more 'Indicator(s)') that defines the actual features of each competency that is assessed.

This framework definition is used to map between the various frameworks. A simple mapping of the UCAM terminology and the frameworks that are used in this book is shown in Table 3.1.

Table 3.1 Mapping between UCAM terms and other frameworks

UCAM term	UKSPEC term	INCOSE term	SFIA term	APM term	APMP term
Competency	Competency	Systems Engineering Ability	Skill	Activity	Competence
Competency Area	Generic Competency	Theme	Subcategory and Category	Section	Syllabus Area/Syllabus Group
Level	Threshold	Level	Level	APM Rating and Your Rating	Level

Once the framework definition has been carried out, it means that there is a basic mapping mechanism between any framework that is being used. It is important to map to the generic framework, as it is these generic terms that are used in UCAM and it is the mechanism that allows UCAM to use any framework.

Framework population

The next element in the meta-model that needs to be discussed is that of 'framework population'. The frameworks, as they stand, define all the relevant competencies for a specific area, but there is a lot of information that is not defined, and that is essential for meeting the requirements of an effective assessment. The framework population element must be performed **once per organisation**, or, in the case of large businesses, once per organisational unit. The key elements involved with framework population are shown in Figure 3.2 below.

Figure 3.2 shows the main elements that need to be understood in order to achieve framework population. The term 'population' is used here quite deliberately, as there is a lot of information that is missing from the framework, quite rightly, but which needs to be defined before an assessment can be performed against the framework.

Figure 3.2 The 'framework population' key elements

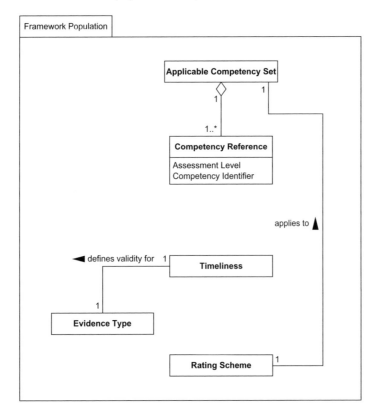

The first of these elements is the 'Applicable Competency Set'. With any of the frameworks used in this book, they are each intended to cover a wide variety of uses in the industry. As such, they will always contain more competencies than are actually useful or necessary for a given business. For example, SFIA has around 80 competencies. There is no way that all of these competencies will be applicable to a single business area and, therefore, it is possible to eliminate some of them from our area of interest. This is what the applicable competency set is designed to do. The idea is to identify the subset of competencies from whichever frameworks are deemed to be useful. Each competency that has been identified is represented in the applicable competency set by a 'Competency Reference' that will be further described by:

- 'Assessment Level', which states the level in the framework to which the competency should be assessed;

- 'Competency Identifier', which is a unique identifier which will allow both the competency and its parent framework to be identified for traceability purposes.

Alongside the applicable competency set lies what is arguably the single most important aspect of the meta-model to get right in order to meet the requirements for assessment – the definition of the 'Evidence Type' for each competency level. The 'Evidence Type' defines what, exactly, can be accepted as valid evidence to demonstrate that the requirements of the level have been met. Consider the case where a four-level framework, such as the INCOSE framework, is being used. For each of the levels, it is important to decide what type of evidence may be acceptable, for example:

1. For level one, 'Awareness', it may be decided that the individual need only demonstrate a knowledge of the key concepts to meet the requirements. The format of this evidence may be verbal confirmation that the concepts are understood – tacit knowledge.

2. For level two, 'Supervised Practitioner', however, it may be deemed necessary to show some experience of having carried out the relevant activities and maybe also to demonstrate that they have undergone some training in the area. The format of this evidence may be artefacts from the processes and a certificate of attendance from a course.

3. For level three, 'Practitioner', it may be decided that it is necessary to hold a formal qualification and to have led a team in the area. The format of this evidence may be artefacts from processes, ownership of artefacts and a formal certificate of qualification.

4. For level four, 'Expert', it may be decided that the individual must have defined process or policy and be an acknowledged expert in the appropriate field or industry. This may also include some professional qualification. The format of this evidence may be documented evidence of having decided policy and process, published articles and presentation on the industry and maybe the achievement of chartered status.

This may seem quite reasonable and straightforward, but there are many subtleties and complexities to defining these evidence types.

- The evidence types may change depending on the size of the organisation. Consider an organisation with over a thousand employees. Being recognised as the organisational guru in a specific field may be enough to attain 'Expert' status, whereas in a company with only five employees this is not necessarily the case at all. In the larger organisation, in-house publications, such as white papers, may be enough to demonstrate expertise, whereas in the smaller organisation, maybe the publication would have to be at conferences or public events.

- The evidence types may have a certain time when they may be considered relevant. This is represented in Figure 3.2 as 'Timeliness'. Consider the idea of a qualification and whether it is a formal degree or attendance of a training course. What timeliness is relevant for each? In the case of the degree, one would hope that it would be relevant for a lifetime, otherwise we would spend most of our lives studying at universities if they had a timeliness of five years. But what about a training course? These tend to be more technology driven; therefore, can we put a timeliness of one, two or three years on one? Likewise, what about someone who attends a course, yet never practises the knowledge taught? Should the evidence of attendance of a training course in this instance be the same as someone who uses the techniques on a daily basis? Clearly, there should be some way to tie in the qualification with practice, but again this complicates the whole issue of evidence types.

- The academic issue. One very serious issue arises when someone reaches the 'Expert' level. There is a train of thought that says that to hold any level, then that person must have attained the level below. However, a very real situation arises when someone reaches a very high level and is dictating policy, writing papers, speaking at conferences, and so on. But is that person still carrying out the day-to-day activities of levels two and three? The answer is probably 'no', but does this mean that they should not be allowed to attain level four? Again, the more thought that is put into a subject like this, the more complex the whole situation becomes.

- The issue of role types. The different roles a person holds in an organisation will mean that the evidence types and associated timeliness will change. For example, someone who is involved with training may have a need to be expert in a particular technology, as may someone who is involved with defining process in this area. The trainer, however, may have a different timeliness, as they need to be fully aware of the exact changes over time of a new technology and never be more than a month or so out of date. With someone who is defining process, however, this may be more lax and have a timeliness set of, say, six months or even a year.

The points raised here should enforce the point that defining the evidence types is certainly non-trivial and cannot be undertaken lightly. There is also the issue that whatever evidence types are decided upon, it is important that other organisations recognise these as being valid. An example of how the applicable competency set and the related evidence can be realised is by using a simple table, as shown in Figure 3.3.

Figure 3.3 shows an example of how an applicable competency set can be visualised. It should be noted that this is a **generic** applicable competency set that

Figure 3.3 Example 'Generic Applicable Competency Set'

Level	Generic applicable competency set								Evidence type
Expert	Professional qualification, publication, activity definition	Professional qualification, publication, activity definition	Professional qualification, publication, activity definition	Professional qualification, publication, activity definition	Professional qualification, publication, activity definition	Professional qualification, publication, activity definition	Professional qualification, publication, activity definition	Professional qualification, publication, activity definition	Professional qualification, publication, activity definition
Practitioner	Educational qualification, lead activity	Educational qualification, lead activity	Educational qualification, lead activity	Educational qualification, lead activity	Educational qualification, lead activity	Educational qualification, lead activity	Educational qualification, lead activity	Educational qualification, lead activity	Educational qualification, lead activity
Supervised practitioner	Formal course, activity	Formal course, activity	Formal course, activity	Formal course, activity	Formal course, activity	Formal course, activity	Formal course, activity	Formal course, activity	Formal course, activity
Awareness	Informal course, tacit knowledge	Informal course, tacit knowledge	Informal course, tacit knowledge	Informal course, tacit knowledge	Informal course, tacit knowledge	Informal course, tacit knowledge	Informal course, tacit knowledge	Informal course, tacit knowledge	Informal course, tacit knowledge
Theme	Systems thinking	Holistic life cycle view						Systems engineering management	
Competency	Systems concepts	Super-system capability issues	Determining and managing stakeholder requirements	Integration and verification	Validation	Functional analysis	Modelling and simulation	Life cycle process definition	Planning, monitoring and controlling

is simply showing the form that an applicable competency set can take. A simple table is used with the competencies along the horizontal axis, and the levels on the vertical axis. The example here is using the INCOSE competency framework, therefore the horizontal axis has the 'Theme' and 'Competency' labelled, whereas the vertical axis has the 'Level' labelled. Each cell in the table features 'Evidence Type'. It should be pointed out that this table has the same evidence type defined for each cell at the same level, but this need not be the case. For example, it may be decided that the evidence types for the same level, but different competencies, will be different. There will be examples of this shown in the case studies.

The final element in the 'Framework definition' is that of the 'Rating Scheme'. When carrying out an assessment, as opposed to an audit, it is important that the result obtained can be used in a useful and pragmatic way. Therefore, assessments will often have a graded output, rather than a simple 'pass or fail' output that is typical of an audit. What this means in reality is that there will be a graded scale, such as:

- 'Fully met' – where all, or the vast majority, of the indicators have been demonstrated. Obtaining this result means that enough evidence has been demonstrated to achieve the level;

- 'Largely met' – where a large proportion of the indicators have been met. Obtaining this result means that not enough evidence has been demonstrated to achieve the level, but that the individual is not far away;

- 'Partially met' – where a smaller proportion of the indicators has been met. Obtaining this result means that not enough evidence has been demonstrated to achieve the level and that the individual still has quite a lot of room for improvement;

- 'Not met' – where no, or very few, of the indicators have been met. Obtaining this rating means that the individual has not really made any progress on achieving the level and that the individual still has a long way to go before achieving the level.

There is no reason why only four levels of achievement should be defined, but this seems to be a number that is good enough to get meaningful results, without being too complex.

The 'Rating Scheme' basically states what percentage of the indicators must be met to obtain that level. A good starting point to use when defining these ratings is shown in Table 3.2:

Table 3.2 Example rating scheme

Rating level	Percentage of indicators required
Fully met	86–100
Largely met	56–85
Partially met	16–55
Not met	0–15

The figures shown in Table 3.2 are recommended as a starting point but are to be used as a guide only. There are some important points to bear in mind when deciding on what these levels will be.

- How harsh do you want to be for 'Not met'? Bear in mind that if the upper boundary for this rating is too high, then many people may be classed as not achieving the level at all. This can have an impact on confidence if people achieve (or under-achieve) this rating.

- Conversely, how generous do you want to be for 'Fully met'? If the lower boundary is set too low, then it will be very easy for people to achieve each level and, hence, will dumb down the achievement of obtaining a full level. In the same way, if the lower boundary is set too high, then few people will ever achieve the level.

- Number of framework indicators. This is, maybe, the single biggest issue when it comes to defining the levels. The number of indicators in a single framework can vary considerably, for example, in the INCOSE framework there are some competencies with upwards of 12 indicators, whereas others have as few as one or two indicators. In the case of having 12 indicators, this is not a problem and will provide a good range of percentages that can be achieved as the increments will be in steps of 8.25 per cent. Looking at the cases where the number of indicators is only two, then this leads to a problem, as the only results obtainable are 0 per cent, 50 per cent or 100 per cent, which is not a good range of results.

The framework population element of the meta-model is absolutely crucial to get right and one with a surprising level of complexity. It can take a lot of time and effort to get this right but this is a necessary evil as, if this is not carried out properly, there will be no rigour in the results of any assessments and the requirements for competency assessment as introduced in the previous chapter will not be met.

Assessment Set-up

Once the framework definition and framework population elements have been defined, then the 'Assessment Set-up' element can be considered. The assessment set-up element needs to be defined **once per set of assessments** to be performed. The main element that needs to be defined here is the 'Competency Scope' and can be seen in Figure 3.4.

Figure 3.4 The Assessment set-up element

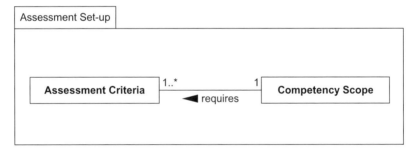

Figure 3.4 shows that the 'Competency Scope' requires one or more 'Assessment Criteria'. The 'Competency Scope' is the main input to any assessment and defines the following information:

- The actual competencies to be assessed. These will be taken from the 'Applicable Competency Set' that has already been defined. This will be a set of competencies that will form the basis of the assessments.

- The level to which each competency will be assessed. This level will come from the 'Framework Definition' and states the maximum level that needs to be assessed. This is important as, in many cases, there is absolutely no value in assessing up to the top level of competency. Indeed, it can be very intimidating and lower morale if people are constantly being assessed to a level which they have no hope of achieving.

- The evidence types that are required at each level. This will come directly from the 'Framework Population' element.

This information can be realised in any way, but a good way to visualise this information is through using a simple table as shown in Figure 3.5.

The example shown in Figure 3.5 shows a simple competency scope for a specific role – in this case a requirements engineer. This chart bears a striking resemblance to Figure 3.3 because it is, in essence, a variation on that diagram. The difference between the two is that the competency scope is indicated by the shaded area on the chart. Note that the shading indicates both which competencies are to be assessed and also the level to which they should be assessed. Once the assessment set-up element has been considered, then the only element remaining is that of the assessment.

Figure 3.5 Example competency scope

Scope – requirements engineer

	Systems concepts	Super-system capability issues	Determining and managing stakeholder requirements	Integration and verification	Validation	Functional analysis	Modelling and simulation	Life cycle process definition	Planning, monitoring and controlling
Expert	Professional qualification, publication, activity definition	Professional qualification, publication, activity definition	Professional qualification, publication, activity definition	Professional qualification, publication, activity definition	Professional qualification, publication, activity definition	Professional qualification, publication, activity definition	Professional qualification, publication, activity definition	Professional qualification, publication, activity definition	Professional qualification, publication, activity definition
Practitioner	Educational qualification, lead activity	Educational qualification, lead activity	Educational qualification, lead activity	Educational qualification, lead activity	Educational qualification, lead activity	Educational qualification, lead activity	Educational qualification, lead activity	Educational qualification, lead activity	Educational qualification, lead activity
Supervised practitioner	Formal course, activity	Formal course, activity	Formal course, activity	Formal course, activity	Formal course, activity	Formal course, activity	Formal course, activity	Formal course, activity	Formal course, activity
Awareness	Informal course, tacit knowledge	Informal course, tacit knowledge	Informal course, tacit knowledge	Informal course, tacit knowledge	Informal course, tacit knowledge	Informal course, tacit knowledge	Informal course, tacit knowledge	Informal course, tacit knowledge	Informal course, tacit knowledge
	Systems thinking		Holistic life cycle view					Systems engineering management	

Assessment

The 'Assessment' element is concerned with performing the actual assessment itself and needs to be carried out **once per assessment**. The main elements of 'Assessment' are shown in Figure 3.6.

Figure 3.6 The 'Assessment' element

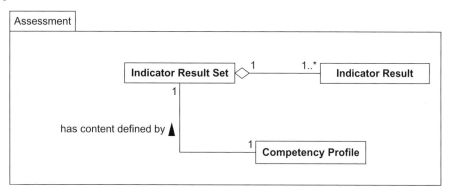

Figure 3.6 shows that the main element is the 'Indicator Result Set' that is made up of one or more 'Indicator Result(s)'. The 'Indicator Result Set' represents the full set of each individual 'Indicator Result'. Each 'Indicator Result' represents a 'pass' or 'fail' result that shows whether or not an indicator has been met. An example of how the indicator set may be realised is shown in Table 3.3.

Table 3.3 Example of an 'Indicator Result Set'

Competency reference: 'System concepts', level 1				Rating scheme	
Indicator	**Evidence type**	**Evidence**	**Pass and Fail**	**% range**	**Level rating**
Is aware of system life cycle	Informal course, tacit knowledge	Formal course certificate	Pass	81%–100%	Fully met
Is aware of hierarchy of systems	Informal course, tacit knowledge	No evidence	Fail	56%–80%	Largely met
Is aware of system context	Informal course, tacit knowledge	No evidence	Fail	**11%–55%**	**Partially met**
Is aware of interfaces	Informal course, tacit knowledge	Informal course certificate	Pass	0%–10%	Not met
		Rating	**50%**		

Table 3.3 shows how an 'Indicator Result Set' may be visualised. The elements in the table are as follows:

- 'Indicator', each of which is identified by the competencies in the scope and taken from the source framework. Therefore, 'is aware of system life cycle' and the other indicators are copied verbatim from the source standard;

- 'Evidence Type', which is identified and taken from the scope. The evidence types, it should be remembered, are defined by the organisation performing the assessment;

- 'Evidence', which is recorded during the interview and forms a formal record of the actual evidence presented by the candidate. All the evidence is captured from the assessee during the interview;

- 'Pass/fail', which is the assessor's verdict on whether the candidate has presented enough evidence to meet this indicator. It is important at this point that a 'pass or fail' decision is made as, if the result is granulated (for example, 'largely met', and such like), the whole assessment becomes very complex. The theory behind this is that if there are enough indicators, then a fair percentage representation of the overall rating can be calculated very simply. If there are very few indicators, then this can become problematic. For similar pragmatic reasons, the use of weighting for particular indicators (for example, one indicator may be deemed to be worth twice as much as another) is not used in this decision. Theoretically, there is nothing to stop someone producing either a granulated or weighted set of indicators, but be aware of the complexity of the calculations;

- 'Rating', which is a simple percentage of indicators passed versus indicators failed;

- 'Rating scheme', which shows percentage levels and, hence, to what degree the competency has been met.

All of the information in the 'Indicator Result Set' may be collected into a 'Competency Profile' that forms the main output of the whole assessment process. An example of how a competency profile may be visualised is shown in Figure 3.7. Again, the chart should look familiar as it is another variation on the charts shown in Figures 3.3 and 3.5. This time, however, the actual level that was achieved is shown as the shaded area, whereas the original competency scope is shown as the thick, black line. It should be immediately apparent where the gaps are between the competency scope (the assessment input) and the competency profile (the assessment output).

BRINGING IT ALL TOGETHER – THE UCAM META-MODEL

All of the four main elements that have been discussed may now be brought together in the form of the UCAM meta-model, which is shown in Figure 3.8.

Figure 3.8 shows how the four main elements may be brought together but, very importantly, it shows the relationships between these elements. By relating the various elements together, the meta-model starts to enforce consistency between the different elements and makes the whole approach start to make sense.

The key relationships are as follows:

- The 'Applicable Competency Set' identifies one or more 'Competency(ies)'. This requirement forms the cornerstone of the whole assessment as it means that each competency in the applicable competency set comes from a source framework somewhere.
- Each 'Indicator' is demonstrated by one or more 'Evidence Type(s)'. This relationship ties together the definition of the evidence types with the indicators that are measured as part of the assessment.
- The 'Competency Scope' applies to the 'Applicable Competency Set'. It is essential that the competency scope, one of the main inputs to the actual assessments, is taken from the applicable competency set.
- The 'Rating Scheme' classifies the relationships between 'Competency Profile' and 'Indicator Result Set'. Notice that this defines the nature of the relationship between the two concepts.
- The 'Indicator Result Set' is directly related to the 'Indicator Set', as it records the results associated with each indicator.
- The 'Indicator Result' is directly related to the 'Indicator', as it records the result for each individual indicator.

Figure 3.7 Example competency profile

	Systems concepts	Super-system capability issues	Determining and managing stakeholder requirements	Integration and verification	Validation	Functional analysis	Modelling and simulation	Life cycle process definition	Planning, monitoring and controlling
Competency profile									
Expert	Not met	Not met	Not met	Not met	Not met	Not met	Not met	Not met	Not met
Practitioner	Not met	Not met	Partially met	Not met	Not met	Not met	Partially met	Not met	Not met
Supervised practitioner	Partially met	Largely met	Fully met	Partially met	Partially met	Partially met	Fully met	Not met	Partially met
Awareness	Partially met	Fully met	Fully met	Fully met	Not met	Fully met	Fully met	Not met	Largely met
	Systems thinking		Holistic life cycle view					Systems engineering management	

Figure 3.8 The UCAM meta-model

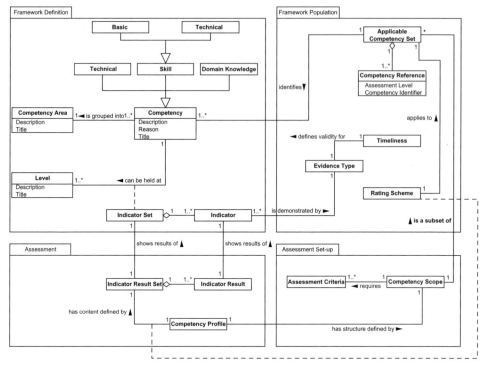

The combination of all these elements, along with their relationships, forms the UCAM meta-model that will be used as a basis for the UCAM assessment process, which will be fully described in the next chapter.

Process automation and tools

As with any process, if it is fully understood and defined, then it is possible to automate that process in an attempt to simplify the process and make it more efficient. In recent years, there have been a great many software applications that have been designed to make our lives easier, in terms of carrying out processes and assessments. These may be thought of as being in the following categories.

- Process automation tools. There are many tools on the market that allow processes to be automated to a certain extent. Consider a process that is defined in terms of its activities (what is done), the activities (what is produced or consumed) and the responsibilities (the stakeholders). A typical process automation tool will guide the user through the various activities, indicate which stakeholder should be involved and provide templates for the artefacts. This is all well and good, but it is essential not to confuse automating a process in terms of guiding someone through it, and actually performing that process. A process automation tool will allow any processes to be automated, but will not capture results. In the event that the tool is to be used to capture the results of an assessment, then assessment tools need to be considered.

- Assessment tools. These are tools that actually execute a specific assessment process. There is a plethora of such tools that are related to process assessment, but not nearly as many as there are related to competency assessment. A process assessment tool will actually do more than guide a user through the process, but will actually capture the data, analyse the data (in some cases) and present the results in charts, tables and so on.

It is important when considering tools that the right one is chosen to suit your individual requirements. Remember, the main key difference is that process automation tools will allow any process to be automated, but will not capture results or do anything clever. Assessment tools will usually execute a specific process but will capture results, analyse them, visualise them, and so on.

Competent assessors

One of the key considerations for pragmatic assessment comes down to the competence of the assessors themselves. There are some core areas where the assessors will require specific competencies:

- In the process. In the case of this book, the assessor would need to be completely familiar with the relevant UCAM processes, how they work, how to capture results, and so on. The word relevant should be stressed here, as, depending on which of the assessor roles will be taken, they may need to be familiar with a different set of processes.

- In the relevant competency framework. The assessors must have an understanding of the source framework that is being assessed against. This can be covered in part by the 'Framework Definition' process in UCAM, which is geared towards generating an understanding of any relevant source framework.

- In the appropriate domain. Whoever is carrying out the assessment must have appropriate domain knowledge. It is not enough to read and understand the source frameworks as the information in them is open to misinterpretation and, therefore, an expert decision may need to be made to clear up any ambiguities.

The obvious answer to how this can be achieved is to define a competency scope for the assessor roles and ensure that anyone involved in assessment holds the appropriate levels of competence. There are three main categories of skills required, as discussed in the previous list, and the following levels are recommended.

The table here shows the levels required for each of the three skill areas discussed previously. These levels are based on a four-level system, such as has been used in several examples throughout this book.

Table 3.4 Suggested scope levels

	Primary assessor	Secondary assessor
UCAM process	Level 3	Level 2
Framework understanding	Level 2	Level 2
Domain knowledge	Level 3	Level 2

CONCLUSIONS

Summary of the elements

There are four main elements that need to be considered for a generic assessment process, and they are:

- the framework definition, where source frameworks are understood and mapped to other frameworks;

- the framework population, where an applicable competency set is defined along with the evidence types that are to be accepted at each level;

- the assessment set-up, where the major assessment inputs, such as the assessment scope, are defined;

- the assessment, where the assessments themselves are carried out, the results captured and a profile produced.

In reality, there will be a number of processes that are executed to realise these elements and this will be the focus of the next chapter, where the core set of UCAM processes will be identified and described.

REFERENCES

Capability Maturity Model Integrated (CMMI) suite of documents, including: (2006) 'CMMI for Development, Version 1.2' (pdf). *CMMI-DEV (Version 1.2, August 2006)*. Carnegie Mellon University Software Engineering Institute. www.sei.cmu.edu/library/abstracts/reports/06tr008.cfm (Accessed February 2011).

(2007) 'CMMI for Acquisition, Version 1.2' (pdf). *CMMI-ACQ (Version 1.2, November 2007)*. Carnegie Mellon University Software Engineering Institute. www.sei.cmu.edu/library/abstracts/reports/07tr017.cfm (Accessed February 2011).

(2007) 'CMMI for Services, Version 1.2' (pdf). *CMMI-SVC (Version 1.2, February 2009)*. Carnegie Mellon University Software Engineering Institute. www.sei.cmu.edu/library/abstracts/reports/09tr001.cfm (Accessed February 2011).

Holt, J. (2009) *A pragmatic guide to business process modelling,* second edition. BCS, the Chartered Institute for IT, Swindon.

ISO (2003) 15288 – systems engineering life-cycle processes.

Software Process Improvement and Capability dEtermination (SPICE). See ISO 15504 – Software process assessment suite of documents, parts 1 to 7 www.iso.org (Accessed February 2011).

Office of Government Commerce (2009) *Managing successful projects with PRINCE II,* fifth edition. Stationery Office Books, London.

4 THE UNIVERSAL COMPETENCY ASSESSMENT MODEL (UCAM) PROCESSES

'Have no fear' said the cat. 'I will not let you fall. I will hold you up high as I stand on the ball. With a book in one hand! And a cup on my hat! But that is not all I can do' said the cat
The Cat in the Hat, Dr Seuss

INTRODUCTION

In Chapter 3 the UCAM was introduced in terms of the common elements relating to competency assessments that must be generated in order to set up and conduct assessments and are produced as outputs from assessments. But how and when are these elements produced and used? This chapter answers this question by looking at the **processes** that form part of the definition of the UCAM.

The importance of modelling

At the heart of the UCAM is a set of four core processes that defines what needs to be done in order to undertake competency assessments using the UCAM approach. These processes are described in the remainder of this chapter using a model-based approach to understanding processes that is described fully in Holt (2009). While this book does not aim to teach modelling, is it worth, before looking at the UCAM processes, considering the question of why bother with modelling at all?

Processes are complex entities, even those that **appear** to be simple. Identifying **what** has to be done does not give a clear picture of a process. How is the work that has to be carried out in a process to be broken down? Who is responsible for carrying out the activities of a process? In what order are the activities carried out and how does the person carrying them out know what to do next? What information is needed before a process can be executed and what information does a process produce? How are these process inputs and outputs related? Why is the process being carried out and how does it relate to other processes?

All of these questions highlight issues of complexity that are inherent in all processes. This complexity can make processes difficult to understand, often leading to mistakes in carrying them out. It can also make it very hard to communicate effectively about processes. This can be particularly problematical when such communication needs to take place between organisations. Different organisations speak different languages – each will have its own specific set of terms for the concepts surrounding processes that forms a barrier to communication and, again, can cause problems if such processes have to be understood and carried out cooperatively by people from multiple organisations. The same problem can even occur **within** organisations, particularly large organisations, where different business units may not even speak the same organisational language.

These three issues of complexity, lack of understanding and communication problems form a vicious triangle, feeding into one another. Unmanaged complexity will lead to a lack of understanding and communication problems. Communication problems will lead to unidentified complexity and a lack of understanding. A lack of understanding will lead to communication problems and complexity. One way to tackle these three 'evils' is to take a 'model-based' approach.

A model-based approach helps us when understanding, defining, documenting and deploying processes. This modelling allows us to identify the complexity in the processes, aid in our understanding of the processes and improve communication about them, and all in a way that uses an established notation within a defined approach to ensure that we are producing a complete, concise and, above all, consistent model of the processes.

Modelling is, in its essence, an approach that allows us to look at any system (in this case, processes) from different points of view, to simplify each view and to ensure that all of these views are consistent. The approach taken here uses a visual notation, in that it uses diagrams, to express any information related to a set of processes.

THE UCAM PROCESSES – AN INTRODUCTION

This section introduces the processes that form part of the UCAM. These processes show how and when the various UCAM elements are produced and used. The approach used here to describe the UCAM processes is known as the 'seven views' approach and makes use of a diagramming notation called the UML. As stated above, this book is not one on learning modelling and the reader is referred to Holt (2009) for a description of the seven views approach and the notation used.

The UCAM requirements
Before looking at the UCAM processes, it is worth, as in any endeavour, looking first at the specific requirements for UCAM and its processes. When considering requirements, we are really asking ourselves the fundamental question 'why are we doing this in the first place?' It is essential to know why we are interested in competency assessment, as different people's needs may be different, hence their requirements may be different. These requirements are shown in Figure 4.1, where each ellipse on the diagram represents a requirement, or need.

The main UCAM requirement is to be able to 'Assess competency' which, if it is to be met, includes requirements to 'Understand source framework', 'Populate framework', Set-up assessment' and 'Carry out assessment'. In order to 'Understand source framework', then there are additional requirements that have to be met to be able to 'Model source framework' and to 'Map source framework to generic framework'. Competency assessments are not carried out for their own sake (or, at least, *should* not be carried out for their own sake) and so the requirement to 'Assess competency' has a number of variants, showing the need to be able to 'Assess competency for accreditation', 'Assess competency for education', 'Assess competency for recruitment', 'Assess competency for staff appraisal' and 'Assess competency for self-assessment'.

Figure 4.1 The UCAM Requirements

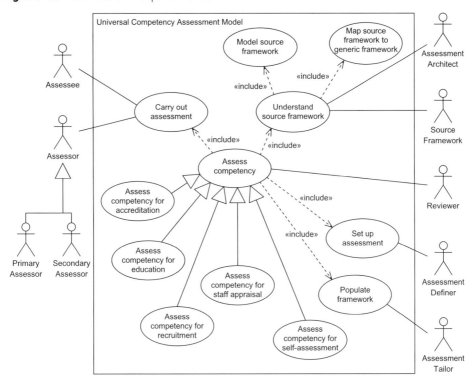

It is no coincidence that the four main areas of UCAM, as discussed in Chapter 3, were concerned with understanding any source frameworks to be used (the framework definition elements), populating the frameworks to be used with the information needed to enable them to be used (the framework population elements), determining the reason and scope for an assessment (the assessment set-up elements) and carrying out the assessment (the assessment elements). These four areas and, as will be seen below, the UCAM processes exist in order to meet the four main UCAM requirements that make up the requirement to 'Assess competency', that is, they exist to meet the requirements to 'Understand source framework', 'Populate framework', 'Set-up assessment' and 'Carry out assessment'.

The UCAM stakeholders

Figure 4.1 also shows the **stakeholders** involved in UCAM. These are represented by the 'stick person' symbols on the diagram, with lines joining each stakeholder to the requirement with which they have an interest. But just **what** is meant by the term 'stakeholder'? A stakeholder represents the **role** of anyone or **anything** that has a vested interest in a project, and can range from an end-user to shareholders in an organisation, to the government of a particular nation. For competency assessments, the important roles are those associated with the definition and carrying out of assessments.

The use of the word 'role' must be emphasised here, as the biggest mistake made by people when defining stakeholders is that they refer to stakeholders by individual names, such as the name of a person or an organisation. It is the **role** of the person or organisation, rather than the actual name, which is of interest from the modelling point of view. For a full discussion of stakeholders, see Holt (2009) or Holt and Perry (2008).

In order to ensure consistency in the definition of the UCAM processes, the stakeholders can be brought together on a stakeholder view that identifies the stakeholders, groups them by type and can, if needed, be used to show any other relationships between the stakeholders. Such a diagram can be seen in Figure 4.2.

Figure 4.2 The UCAM Stakeholders

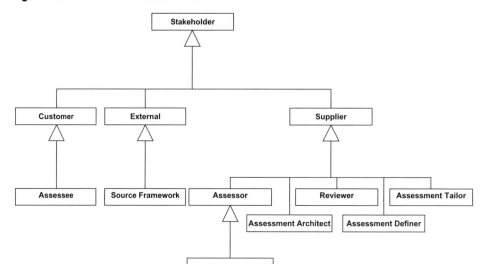

Figure 4.2 shows that there are three main types of 'Stakeholder': 'Customer', 'External' and 'Supplier'. These are chosen as the highest-level stakeholders, as almost every project will have both a supplier and a customer and will normally have some external stakeholders such as standards or legislation.

The 'Customer' stakeholder represents those stakeholders that are the recipients of the service being provided, in this case recipients of an assessment. The 'Customer' roles may be influenced by the 'Support' roles in certain circumstances, but are typically considered as being separate. One specific role is shown:

- 'Assessee'. This role is carried out by the person (or people) being assessed against a competency framework and, as such, who has an interest in the 'Carry out assessment' requirement.

The 'External' stakeholder represents stakeholders such as standards, legislation or external systems. An 'External' role is not usually influenced by either customer or supplier and represents standards, best-practice models or policing roles. One specific role is shown for the 'External' stakeholder role:

- 'Source Framework'. This role represents any source frameworks against which assessments will be carried out and is therefore linked to the 'Understand source framework' requirement. Note that this stakeholder very much represents a 'thing', in this case a document, rather than a person or organisation. This is a perfectly valid, though often overlooked, use of stakeholders.

The 'Supplier' stakeholder represents those stakeholders who are involved in the supply of a service, in this case those stakeholders involved in carrying out an assessment. The 'Supplier' role has five specific roles shown:

- 'Assessor'. This role is broken down into two specific assessor roles, those of 'Primary Assessor' and 'Secondary Assessor'. These roles are typically carried out by the people (although in years to come, this role could be taken by a computer application), as discussed later in this chapter, responsible for conducting an assessment. The 'Assessor' role is therefore linked to the 'Carry out assessment' requirement.

- 'Assessment Architect'. This role is carried out by the person (or people) responsible for the understanding of source frameworks and their mapping to the generic UCAM meta-model, as described by the 'Understand source framework' requirement.

- 'Assessment Tailor'. This role is carried out by the person (or people) responsible for tailoring the source frameworks in order to establish the framework against which assessments will be conducted. The role is, therefore, linked to the 'Populate framework' requirement.

- 'Assessment Definer'. This role represents the person (or people) responsible for establishing the needs for a particular set of assessments that are to be carried out. That is, for ensuring that the requirement to 'set-up assessment' is met.

- 'Reviewer'. This role represents the person (or people) responsible for ensuring that the definition, set-up and carrying out of assessments is conducted correctly and as such has an interest in all of the UCAM requirements. This is shown by their link to the main 'Assess competency' requirement.

One of the reasons why we consider **roles** when discussing stakeholders, rather than names, is that the names may change, but the roles remain the same. Consider the situation where a self-assessment is being carried out by someone in a very small company. In such a situation, it may be possible that a single person takes on **all** roles in the customer and supplier categories. Imagine another situation where a large organisation intends to assess a thousand employees, then it is totally unfeasible for a single person to take on each role – especially the assessors. The exact responsibilities of these stakeholder roles, in terms of the activities to be carried out in the UCAM processes, will be discussed below when each of the UCAM processes is discussed.

The UCAM processes

In order to meet the requirements discussed above and to support the concepts described in Chapter 3, four UCAM processes and a number of supporting processes have been defined. These processes are shown in Figure 4.3.

Figure 4.3 The UCAM Processes

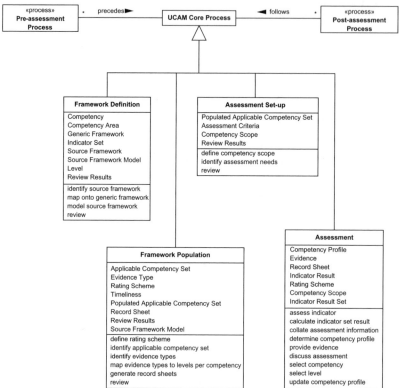

Figure 4.3 shows that the four types of 'UCAM Core Process' are the 'Framework Definition' process, 'Framework Population' process, 'Assessment Set-up' process and 'Assessment' process. As discussed above, each of these processes is responsible for the production and utilisation of the UCAM elements relating to one area of the UCAM meta-model described in Chapter 3 and, hence, for fulfilling the main UCAM requirements introduced in 'The UCAM requirements' section above. Thus, for example, the 'Framework Definition' process is responsible for meeting the requirement to 'Understand source framework' and for the production and utilisation of the elements described in the 'Framework Definition' part of the UCAM meta-model.

Figure 4.3 also shows what has to be done in each process (the **activities** that have to be carried out, shown in the bottom compartment of each process) and what things are either produced by or consumed by each process (the **artefacts** that flow into or out of the process, shown in the middle compartment). It does not attempt to show how each process is carried out. This description of **process behaviour**, together with a detailed discussion of each process, is contained in the four sections which follow.

Before a UCAM process is executed, it may be necessary to precede it with zero or more 'Pre-assessment process(es)'. Similarly, a UCAM process may have to be followed by zero or more 'Post-assessment process(es)'. These non-core UCAM support processes are discussed in 'UCAM support processes' below.

THE FRAMEWORK DEFINITION PROCESS

This section describes the 'Framework Definition' process introduced in 'The UCAM processes' section above and executed in order to understand and model source frameworks.

Requirements for the Framework Definition process

The requirements for the 'Framework Definition' process are given below in Figure 4.4 which highlights the relevant requirements on the diagram introduced in Figure 4.1 above.

Figure 4.4 Requirements for the Framework Definition process

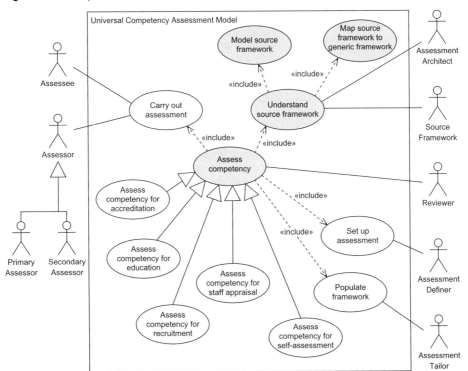

As can be seen in Figure 4.4, the main requirement for the 'Framework Definition' process is to 'Understand source framework', which includes 'Model source framework' and 'Map source framework to generic framework'. The activities that are needed in the process to meet these requirements, and the artefacts that form inputs to and outputs from the process are described in the following section.

Contents of the Framework Definition process

Figure 4.5 defines the contents (but **not** the behaviour) of the 'Framework Definition' process using the 'process content view' technique described in Holt (2009). The process is represented as a rectangle divided into three compartments. The top compartment labelled '«process» Framework Definition' simply identifies the process. The middle compartment identifies the **artefacts** that are inputs **to** and outputs **from** the process, with the «in» and «out» stereotypes indicating the direction of flow for the artefacts. Each artefact has its name shown. The bottom compartment identifies the **activities** that need to be performed in the process. Note that there is **no** implied ordering of the activities and, in fact, activities can run in parallel. The intention here is simply to identify the activities.

Figure 4.5 The contents of the Framework Definition Process

```
«process»
Framework Definition

«out» Competency
«out» Competency Area
«in» Generic Framework
«out» Indicator Set
«out» Source Framework
«out» Source Framework Model
«out» Level
«out» Review Results

identify source framework
map onto generic framework
model source framework
review
```

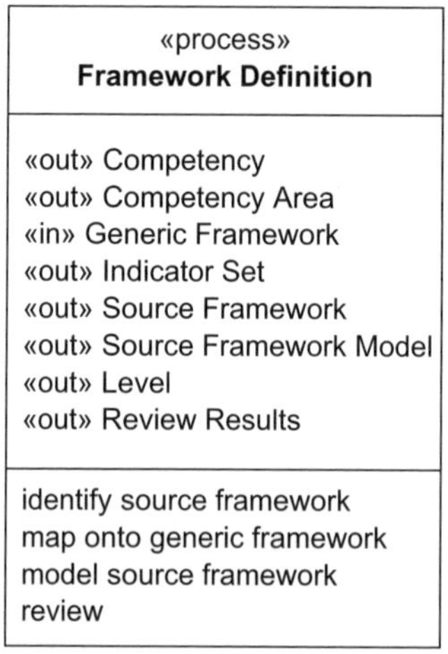

Figure 4.5 shows that there are four activities that have to be carried out in the 'Framework Definition' process, namely 'identify source framework', 'map onto generic framework', 'model source framework' and 'review'. The process produces and consumes the eight artefacts shown. But **how** is the 'Framework Definition' process carried out? This is shown in the following section.

Carrying out the Framework Definition process

The 'Framework Population' process is executed in order to identify the competency frameworks that can be used as a source of competencies against which assessments can be carried out. It also ensures that any such frameworks that have been identified are modelled and mapped onto a generic framework in order to ensure understanding of the concepts found in the source frameworks.

While somewhat time-consuming to run, in terms of the modelling that has to be performed, the 'Framework Definition' process should only require infrequent execution. Once a framework (or frameworks) has been identified and modelled, it only needs revisiting if a new version of the framework is released. Even then, if the changes in the new version are found to be minor, the execution of the 'Framework Definition' process to address these changes may not require much time or effort. Of course, the opposite is also true, should there be major revisions to a source framework.

Figure 4.6 shows how the 'Framework Definition' process is carried out. The 'soft boxes' (rectangles with rounded corners) represent the various activities that have

Figure 4.6 Carrying out the Framework Definition process

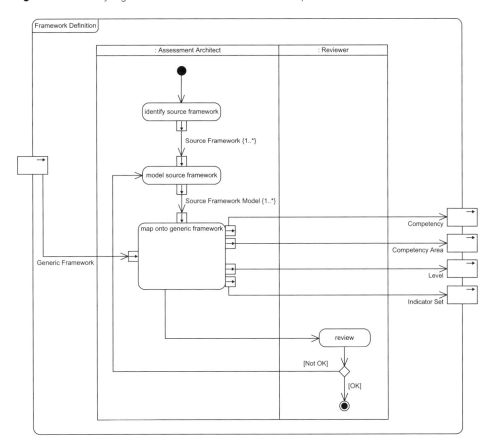

to be carried out and correspond with those shown in the bottom compartment in Figure 4.5. The vertical divisions (swim lanes) indicate which stakeholder role is responsible for carrying out which activity, and correspond to one or more of the stakeholder roles identified in Figure 4.2. The small rectangles containing arrows (known as 'pins') show inputs to and outputs from the various activities, with the name of the artefact flowing into or out of the activity shown on the line connecting the pins. These artefacts correspond to those found in the middle compartment in Figure 4.5.

The 'Framework Definition' process starts with the 'Assessment Architect' carrying out the 'identify source framework' activity in order to identify source competency frameworks that are deemed to be suitable as the basis for competency assessments. This is largely a research activity and the 'Source Framework(s)' output is documentation on the frameworks identified.

Next, the 'Assessment Architect' takes the 'Source Framework(s)' documentation and undertakes the 'model source framework' activity in order to produce a model of each 'Source Framework'. It is suggested that the techniques described in Holt (2009) are used to produce these models.

With the 'Source Framework Model(s)' defined, it is time to carry out the 'map onto generic framework' activity. As well as the 'Source Framework Model' artefacts as input, this activity also uses the 'Generic Framework', a model of the generic competency framework concepts as described in Chapter 3, i.e. the Universal Competency Assessment **Model**. Each concept from a 'Source Framework Model' is mapped onto the corresponding concept, or concepts, from the 'Generic Framework'. In particular, mappings to the generic concepts of 'Competency', 'Competency Area', 'Level' and 'Indicator Set' are essential. This gives an understanding of how the concepts and, particularly, the **vocabulary** used in the 'Source Framework' relates to the generic concepts. The mappings to 'Competency', 'Competency Area', 'Level' and 'Indicator Set' are the main outputs of the 'Framework Definition' process.

Once the 'map onto generic framework' activity is complete, the various generated artefacts are then reviewed in the 'review' activity by the 'Reviewer' role. If there are any problems, then the process repeats from the 'model source framework' activity. If all is okay, the process ends. The various artefacts of the 'Framework Definition' process and their relationships are discussed further in the following section.

Artefacts of the Framework Definition process
The artefacts of the 'Framework Definition' process and their relationships are show in Figure 4.7.

The two main outputs from the 'Framework Definition' process are the documentation on any 'Source Framework' that has been identified as relevant (such as the INCOSE Systems Engineering Competencies Framework or SFIA), and the associated 'Source Framework Model' for each 'Source Framework'. The 'Source Framework Model' will typically be a UML model of the 'Source Framework', although other modelling notations can be used.

Figure 4.7 Relationships between the artefacts of the Framework Definition process

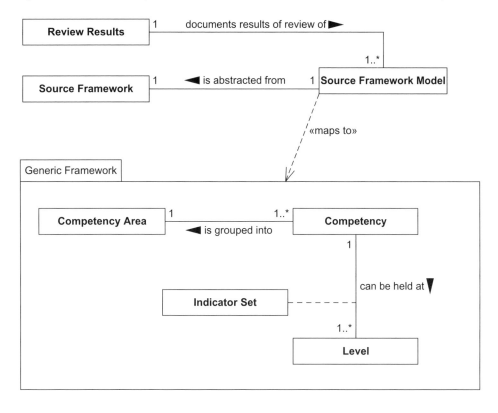

The key point about the 'Source Framework Model' is that it should be mapped to the 'Generic Framework' (itself a model) which abstracts the concepts common to all competency frameworks. In the context of this book, the 'Generic Framework' is, of course, the UCAM.

When carrying out this mapping, it is essential that the 'Source Framework Model' contains mappings to the generic concepts of 'Competency' that represent the concept of something that can be assessed. In order to simplify the use of competency frameworks, most include the concept of 'Competency Area'. This is nothing more than a grouping of related competencies, for example, all those competencies related to process modelling.

'Level' represents the concept that a 'Competency' can typically be held at one of a number of different competency levels. In the source frameworks these may be indicated by a simple numerical indicator, such as 'Level 1' or 'Level 2', or by a more descriptive level name such as 'Awareness Level' or 'Supervised Practitioner Level'.

When determining which 'Level' a given 'Competency' is held at for an assessee, then the 'Indicator Set' is used as the basis of the determination. In most frameworks, each 'Competency' has a number of indicators associated with it. The indicators are the individual items that have to be assessed against for that competency **at a given level**. The 'Indicator Set' is simply the set of such indicators for a given 'Competency' and 'Level'.

Finally, the 'Review Results' artefact is simply a record of the outcome of the 'review' activity that is carried out at the end of the process to ensure that all the generated artefacts, and, in particular, the 'Source Framework Model', are fit for purpose.

Summary of the Framework Definition process

The 'Framework Definition' process exists to allow possible source frameworks to be identified and understood through a process of modelling candidate frameworks and mapping their concepts onto generic competency assessment concepts as embodied in the UCAM meta-model. The key output from the process is a 'Source Framework Model' for each candidate framework.

Discussion on the Framework Definition process

In order to aid the understanding of the source frameworks, the authors have found the most effective approach is to model the frameworks using a modelling language such as the Unified Modelling Language (UML) or the Systems Modelling Language (SysML). The 'seven views' approach that is used in this chapter to document the UCAM processes can also be used to help guide such a modelling activity. See Holt (2009) and Holt and Perry (2008) for information on the 'seven views' and on the SysML. Appendix A gives a very brief overview of the approach. Modelling is essential, as it allows the consistency of source frameworks to be established and it forms the basis for mapping from the source framework to the generic UCAM model in order to understand the terminology, concepts and content of source frameworks. Remember that just because a source framework is backed by a large professional body and published as a set of glossy documents, this does not ensure that the framework is documented and presented in a consistent fashion. Indeed, many international standards are found to be inconsistent when using a model-based approach analysis.

THE FRAMEWORK POPULATION PROCESS

This section describes the 'Framework Population' process introduced in 'The UCAM processes' section above and executed in order to establish the competencies from source frameworks that will be used as a basis of assessment and the evidence that will be accepted to support an assessment.

Requirements for the Framework Population process

The requirements for the 'Framework Population' process are given below in Figure 4.8 which highlights the relevant requirements on the diagram introduced in Figure 4.1 above.

Figure 4.8 Requirements for the Framework Population process

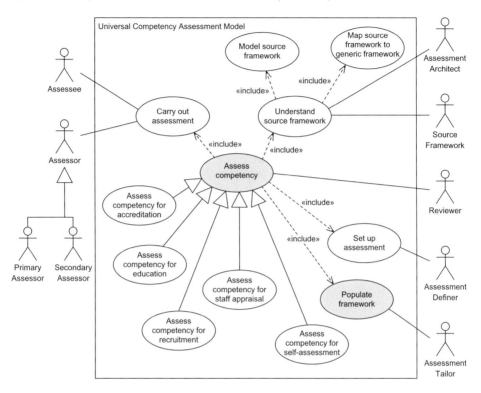

As can be seen in Figure 4.8, the main requirement for the 'Framework Population' process is to 'Populate framework'. The activities that are needed in the process to meet this requirement, and the artefacts that form inputs to and outputs from the process are described in the following section.

Contents of the Framework Population process

The contents of the 'Framework Population' process are shown in Figure 4.9, annotated to show whether the various artefacts are inputs or outputs from the process.

Figure 4.9 shows that there are six activities that have to be carried out in the 'Framework Population' process, namely 'define rating scheme', 'identify applicable competency set', 'identify evidence types', 'map evidence types to levels per competency', 'generate record sheets' and 'review'. The process takes the 'Source Framework Model(s)' output from the 'Framework Definition' process and uses them to generate the other artefacts, such as 'Applicable Competency Set' and 'Evidence Type', that are shown in Figure 4.9. The way that the 'Framework Population' process is carried out is shown in the following section.

Figure 4.9 The contents of the Framework Population process

«process»
Framework Population

«out» Applicable Competency Set
«out» Evidence Type
«out» Rating Scheme
«out» Timeliness
«out» Populated Applicable Competency Set
«out» Record Sheet
«out» Review Results
«in» Source Framework Model

define rating scheme
identify applicable competency set
identify evidence types
map evidence types to levels per competency
generate record sheets
review

Carrying out the Framework Population process

Figure 4.10 shows how the 'Framework Population' process is carried out. The 'soft boxes' (rectangles with rounded corners) represent the various activities that have to be carried out and correspond with those shown in the bottom compartment in Figure 4.9. The vertical divisions (swim lanes) indicate which stakeholder role is responsible for carrying out which activity, and correspond to one or more of the stakeholder roles identified in Figure 4.9. The small rectangles containing arrows (known as 'pins') show inputs to and outputs from the various activities, with the name of the artefact flowing into or out of the activity shown on the line connecting the pins. These artefacts correspond to those found in the middle compartment in Figure 4.9. The two thick horizontal lines at top left indicate that the activities **between** the lines ('identify evidence types', 'define rating scheme', and so on) can conceptually take place in parallel. This region of the diagram looks somewhat complex with all the pins with lines going into them, but simply shows that the 'Source Framework Model' artefact is an input to all three activities in the parallel region.

Figure 4.10 shows that the 'Framework Population' process begins with the 'Assessment Tailor' taking the 'Source Framework Model' artefacts as inputs to the process and undertaking the 'identify evidence types', 'identify applicable competency set' and 'define rating scheme' activities in parallel. These activities are intended to achieve the following:

1. 'identify evidence types'. This activity uses the 'Source Framework Model(s)' to identify the 'Evidence Type(s)' that are deemed to be acceptable to support a

competency assessment. Associated with each 'Evidence Type' is a 'Timeliness' that specifies the acceptable time limits for the validity of a piece of evidence.

2. 'identify applicable competency set'. This activity is executed to identify those competencies from within the 'Source Framework Model(s)' that are deemed to be applicable to the work undertaken by the organisation. If a competency framework contains competencies that are not relevant to an organisation, then there is little point in assessing against them. The 'Applicable Competency Set' that is output by this activity contains just those competencies from the 'Source Framework Model(s)' that are relevant to the organisation.

3. 'define rating scheme'. In order to generate the output from a competency assessment (a 'Competency Profile', discussed in the section on the 'Assessment' process below), it is necessary to be able to convert the simple pass or fail result that is recorded against each competency 'Indicator' into a rating that can be used to generate the 'Competency Profile'. This activity is executed to generate such a 'Rating Scheme'.

Figure 4.10 Carrying out the Framework Population process

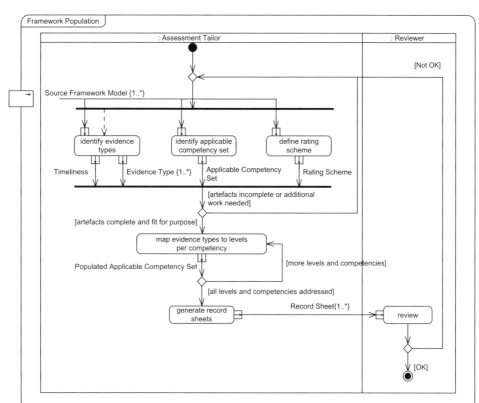

Once these three activities have been completed, a check is made that all are complete and that the various artefacts are fit for purpose. If there are any problems, then the process returns to the beginning and the three activities are repeated. If all is OK, then the 'map evidence types to level per competency' activity is executed. This activity takes the 'Applicable Competency Set' and 'Evidence Type(s)' and assigns an 'Evidence Type' to each competency-level combination for all the competencies in the 'Applicable Competency Set'. The resulting artefact is known as the 'Populated Applicable Competency Set', since it has been populated with relevant 'Evidence Type(s)' and can now be used to help set up assessments, as described in the section below on the 'Assessment Set-up' process. This activity is repeated until all competencies and levels have been addressed. When all have been considered, the 'generate record sheets' activity is executed. This simple activity generates the 'Record Sheet(s)' that is used during an assessment to record the results of the assessment. Finally, the 'review' activity is carried out by the 'Reviewer' in order to check that all the artefacts generated by the process are fit for purpose. If everything is OK, then the process ends. Otherwise, the process restarts. The various artefacts of the 'Framework Population' process and their relationships are discussed further in the following section.

Artefacts of the Framework Population process

The main output from the 'Framework Population' process is the 'Populated Applicable Competency Set' that is used as the basis for the competency scopes generated by the 'Assessment Set-up' process, as described in the discussion of that process below. The artefacts of the 'Framework Population' process and the relationships between them are shown in Figure 4.11.

Figure 4.11 Relationships between the artefacts of the Framework Population process

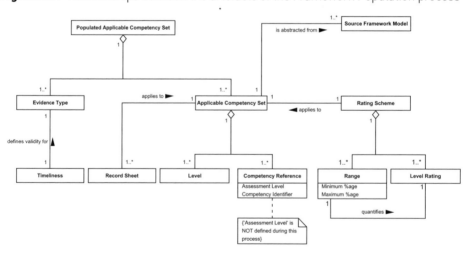

At the heart of the artefacts, as can be seen in Figure 4.11, is the 'Applicable Competency Set'. This is a subset of competencies that are deemed relevant to the organisation as abstracted from the 'Source Framework Model(s)' that form an input to the 'Framework Population' process. The 'Applicable Competency Set' contains these competencies via one or more 'Competency Reference', which is simply a reference to the competency in its source framework. As well as identifying the relevant competencies, the 'Applicable Competency Set' also identifies the maximum 'Level' to which that competency will be assessed in any assessments conducted by the organisation.

In order to capture the results of an assessment, a 'Record Sheet' is needed. This applies to those competencies and levels identified in the 'Applicable Competency Set'. Assessed competencies are rated according to the 'Rating Scheme', an example of which is given in Figure 4.12 below.

Figure 4.12 Example 'Populated Applicable Competency Set'

Level	Generic applicable competency set							Evidence type	
Expert	Professional qualification, publication, activity definition	Professional qualification, publication, activity definition	Professional qualification, publication, activity definition	Professional qualification, publication, activity definition	Professional qualification, publication, activity definition	Professional qualification, publication, activity definition	Professional qualification, publication, activity definition	Professional qualification, publication, activity definition	Professional qualification, publication, activity definition
Practitioner	Educational qualification, lead activity	Educational qualification, lead activity	Educational qualification, lead activity	Educational qualification, lead activity	Educational qualification, lead activity	Educational qualification, lead activity	Educational qualification, lead activity	Educational qualification, lead activity	Educational qualification, lead activity
Supervised practitioner	Formal course, activity	Formal course, activity	Formal course, activity	Formal course, activity	Formal course, activity	Formal course, activity	Formal course, activity	Formal course, activity	Formal course, activity
Awareness	Informal course, tacit knowledge	Informal course, tacit knowledge	Informal course, tacit knowledge	Informal course, tacit knowledge	Informal course, tacit knowledge	Informal course, tacit knowledge	Informal course, tacit knowledge	Informal course, tacit knowledge	Informal course, tacit knowledge
Theme	Systems thinking	Holistic life cycle view						Systems engineering management	
Competency	Systems concepts	Super-system capability issues	Determining and managing stakeholder requirements	Integration and verification	Validation	Functional analysis	Modelling and simulation	Life cycle process definition	Planning, monitoring and controlling

When an 'Applicable Competency Set' is combined with 'Evidence Type', then they together form the 'Populated Applicable Competency Set' that is the main output from the process. An example of a 'Populated Applicable Competency Set' is given in Figure 4.12.

The 'Populated Applicable Competency Set' in Figure 4.12 shows all those competencies that the organisation deems to be relevant the work it undertakes, together with the maximum level to which each competency can be assessed along with the 'Evidence Type' that will be accepted for each competency-level combination. There are a number of points to be noted about the information shown in Figure 4.12:

- All competencies are shown as theoretically capable of being assessed to 'Expert' level, but there is no reason why the maximum level should be the same for all competencies.

- All the competencies shown happen to be from the same source framework, but the whole point of the UCAM approach is that this need not be the case and, in reality, the 'Populated Applicable Competency Set' will contain competencies from a number of different frameworks.

- The same 'Evidence Type' is shown for all competencies at a given level. Again, there is no reason why this needs to be the case.

It is important that the various 'Evidence Type(s)' are clearly understood and that the 'Timeliness' that defines the validity of each type is recorded. A simple example of this is given in Table 4.1.

Table 4.1 Example of 'Evidence Types' and associated 'Timeliness'

Evidence type	Description	Timeliness
Informal course	A training course that is not recognised by a professional body.	2 years
Tacit knowledge	Knowledge that the assessee can demonstrate through conversation.	5 years
Formal course	A training course that is recognised by a professional body.	3 years
Activity	An activity relevant to the competency (or indicator) that the assessee has undertaken under supervision.	2 years
Educational qualification	A qualification recognised by an educational body such as a university.	30 years
Lead activity	An activity relevant to the competency (or indicator) that the assessee has undertaken and for which they have taken a lead role.	3 years
Professional qualification	A qualification granted by a professional body, such as a CEng, CITP.	5 years

(Continued)

Table 4.1 *(Continued)*

Evidence type	Description	Timeliness
Publication	A publication, such as a paper or book, for which the assessee is a main contributor.	5 years (papers and so on) 10 years books
Activity definition	Activities that the assessee has defined, such as organisational process or policy.	5 years

Table 4.1 lists a number of different values for 'Evidence Type', along with a brief description of each. Each 'Evidence Type' also has the validity period, or 'Timeliness' for that 'Evidence Type' shown. The table shows a simple maximum age for each type, but much more complex schemes can be defined, such as having 'Timeliness' depend on the actual competency and level. Of course, this makes the conduct of assessments more difficult and time-consuming.

A 'Rating Scheme' is used during the 'Assessment' process (see below) to convert a percentage calculated from the number of indicators of a competency that are marked as having been passed into a 'Level Rating' that gives a textual description of the degree to which a given competency has been met at a given level. An example 'Rating Scheme' is shown in Table 4.2.

Table 4.2 shows the mapping from percentage to 'Level Rating'. Thus, for a competency with five indicators at a particular level, three of which are considered to have been passed, the 'Rating Scheme' gives a 'Level Rating' of 'Largely met', since the percentage of indicators that have been passed for that competency and level is 60 per cent. The percentages and level ratings shown in Table 4.2 are those that have been found to be most useful by the authors and may not meet the requirements for every organisation.

Table 4.2 Example 'Rating Scheme'

Level rating	Percentage of indicators required
Fully met	86–100
Largely met	56–85
Partially met	16–55
Not met	0–15

Summary of the Framework Population process

The 'Framework Population' process is concerned with defining the 'Populated Applicable Competency Set', 'Evidence Type' and 'Rating Scheme' as appropriate for an organisation or organisational unit such as a business unit or even a project team. These artefacts are the main inputs to the 'Assessment Set-up' process and define those competencies that are relevant to the organisation, the evidence that will be accepted and the rating scheme that will be used to convert the results of an assessment into a 'Competency Profile', as described below in the section on the 'Assessment' process.

Discussion on the Framework Population process

The contents of the populated applicable competency set not only depend on the source frameworks that have been chosen as a basis for competency assessments, but also on the activities carried out by an organisation or organisational unit. There is no point including a competency from a framework in the competency set if it relates to an area of work in which the organisation is **not** involved.

When it comes to defining evidence types, it is necessary to strike a balance between rigour and flexibility. Evidence has to be strong enough to demonstrate that a competency has been met, but too much rigour can make it impossible to run assessments in anything like a reasonable time. It is also important to think about any additional constraints, such as timeliness, that might need to be associated with evidence types.

In order to convert the simple 'pass or fail' marks recorded against each indicator into a graded mark that can be used to generate a competency profile it is necessary to define a rating scheme. When deciding on a rating scheme, it is important to establish the desired granularity of level ratings. Do you want a four-level scheme such as is seen in this book ('not met', 'partially met', 'largely met' and 'fully met'), a three-level scheme, or a six-level scheme? It is essential that the number of indicators for a competency allows achievement of all level ratings. If this is not possible, then the introduction of additional indicators not found in the original framework may be necessary.

Finally, whatever the contents of the applicable competency set, the types of evidence deemed acceptable and the rating scheme defined, it is essential that the population of the framework be validated with those for whom the assessments are being performed.

THE ASSESSMENT SET-UP PROCESS

This section describes the 'Assessment Set-up' process introduced in 'The UCAM Processes' section above and executed in order to set up an assessment or set of assessments.

Requirements for the Assessment Set-up process

The requirements for the 'Assessment Set-up' process are given below in Figure 4.13, which highlights the relevant requirements on the diagram introduced in Figure 4.1 above.

Figure 4.13 Requirements for the Assessment Set-up process

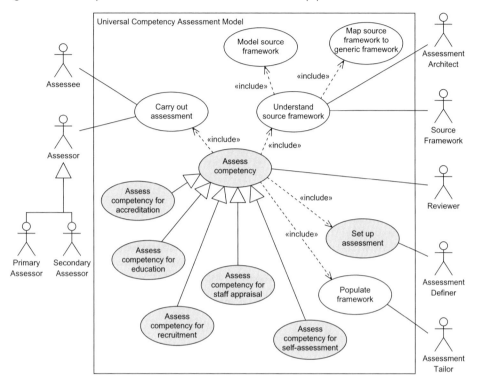

As can be seen in Figure 4.13, the main requirement for the 'Assessment Set-up' process is to 'Set up assessment'. The process must enable assessments to be set up to meet the requirements to be able to 'Assess competency for accreditation', 'Assess competency for education', 'Assess competency for recruitment', 'Assess competency for staff appraisal' and 'Assess competency for self-assessment'. The activities that are needed in the process to meet these requirements, and the artefacts that form inputs to and outputs from the process are described in the following section.

Contents of the Assessment Set-up process
The contents of the 'Assessment Set-up' process are shown in Figure 4.14, annotated to show whether the various artefacts are inputs or outputs from the process.

Figure 4.14 shows that there are three activities that have to be carried out in the 'Assessment Set-up' process, namely 'define competency scope', 'identify assessment needs' and 'review'. The process takes the 'Populated Applicable Competency Set' output from the 'Framework Population' process and uses it to generate the 'Competency Scope(s)' for the assessments. The way that the 'Assessment Set-up' process is carried out is shown in the following section.

Figure 4.14 The contents of the Assessment Set-up process

«process»
Assessment Set-up
«in» Populated Applicable Competency Set
«out» Assessment Criteria
«out» Competency Scope
«out» Review Results
define competency scope
identify assessment needs
review

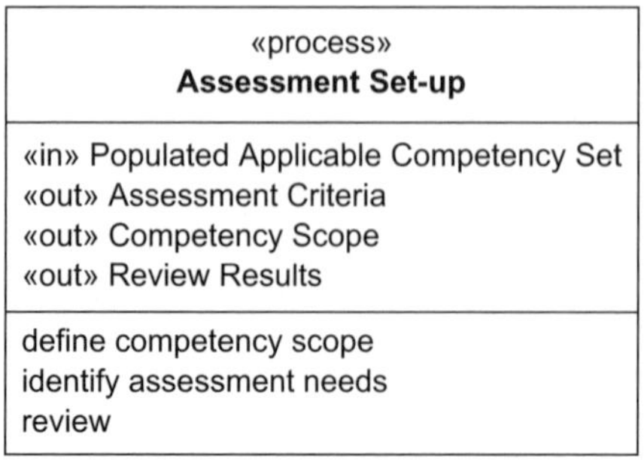

Carrying out the Assessment Set-up process

Figure 4.15 shows how the 'Assessment Set-up' process is carried out. The 'soft boxes' (rectangles with rounded corners) represent the various activities that have to be carried out and correspond to those shown in the bottom compartment in Figure 4.14. The vertical divisions (swim lanes) indicate which stakeholder role is responsible for carrying out which activity, and correspond to one or more of the stakeholder roles identified in Figure 4.2. The small rectangles containing arrows (known as 'pins') show inputs to and outputs from the various activities, with the name of the artefact flowing into or out of the activity shown on the line connecting the pins. These artefacts correspond to those found in the middle compartment in Figure 4.14.

Figure 4.15 shows that the 'Assessment Set-up' process begins with the 'Assessment Definer' carrying out the 'identify assessment needs' activity. This is conducted in order to decide just *why* the assessment or set of assessments is to be conducted and generates the 'Assessment Criteria' containing these reasons.

The 'Assessment Definer' then takes these 'Assessment Criteria' along with the 'Populated Applicable Competency Set' (which the diagram shows is an **input** to this process) and uses them as inputs to the 'define competency scope' activity. Knowing **why** the assessment is to be carried out (the 'Assessment Criteria') and the competencies against which an assessment can be conducted (the 'Populated Applicable Competency Set') enables the 'Competency Scope' to be defined. This scope details the exact competencies against which the assessment will be performed, along with the levels to which each competency will be assessed. Such scopes are often produced for a defined role within an organisation and it is not uncommon for a library of such reusable scopes to be produced by an organisation over time as the process is run a number of times. Eventually, it may be possible to dispense with this process (or, at least, run through it very quickly) once an organisation has such a library of previously defined scopes from which they can pick.

Figure 4.15 Carrying out the Assessment Set-up process

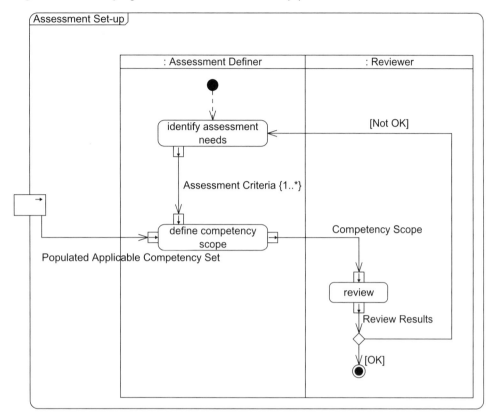

The 'Competency Scope' feeds into the 'review' activity, which is carried out by the 'Reviewer' in order to check that everything is OK with the defined 'Competency Scope'. The results of the review activity are documented in the 'Review Results' artefact. If there are problems with the 'Competency Scope', then the process starts again with the 'identify assessment needs' activity. If there are no problems, then the 'Assessment Set-up' process terminates, having successfully determined the criteria for the assessments and generated the scopes against which the assessments will be carried out. The various artefacts of the 'Assessment Set-up' process and their relationships are discussed further in the following section.

Artefacts of the Assessment Set-up process
The main output from the 'Assessment Set-up' process is the 'Competency Scope' (or scopes) that is to be used as the basis of a set of competency assessments. The artefacts used and produced by the process, along with their relationships, are shown in Figure 4.16.

Figure 4.16 Relationships between the artefacts of the Assessment Set-up process

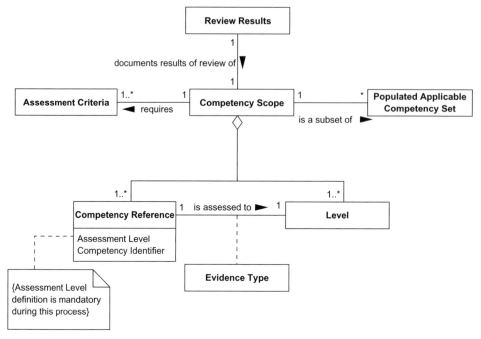

While the main output of the 'Assessment Set-up' process is the 'Competency Scope', this cannot be produced without understanding the reasons for conducting the assessment. These reasons are captured in the 'Assessment Criteria' artefact. This is specified as a formal process artefact deliberately to force the documentation of the criteria to be produced, rather than allowing them to be something that is just thought about and never written down, an all-too-common approach which often leads to consideration of the reasons for an assessment to be skipped, resulting in ill-defined assessments and consequent problems in defining an appropriate scope.

The 'Competency Scope', generated based on these 'Assessment Criteria' is a subset of the 'Populated Applicable Competency Set' described above in the section on the 'Framework Population' process. No assessment can practically assess against every possible competency applicable to an organisation (or even part of an organisation) and so the 'Competency Scope' details just those competencies against which competency will be assessed. It consists of a number of references to competencies from the 'Populated Applicable Competency Set'. Such a reference is represented in the diagram as a 'Competency Reference'. In addition, the 'Level' to which a competency is to be assessed must also be defined together with the 'Evidence Type' that will be accepted when assessing that competency at the indicated level.

Finally, the 'Review Results' artefact is simply a record of the outcome of the 'review' activity that is carried out at the end of the process to ensure that all the generated artefacts, and, in particular, the 'Competency Scope', are fit for purpose.

An example of a 'Competency Scope', first seen in Chapter 3, is given in Figure 4.17.

Figure 4.17 Example 'Competency Scope'

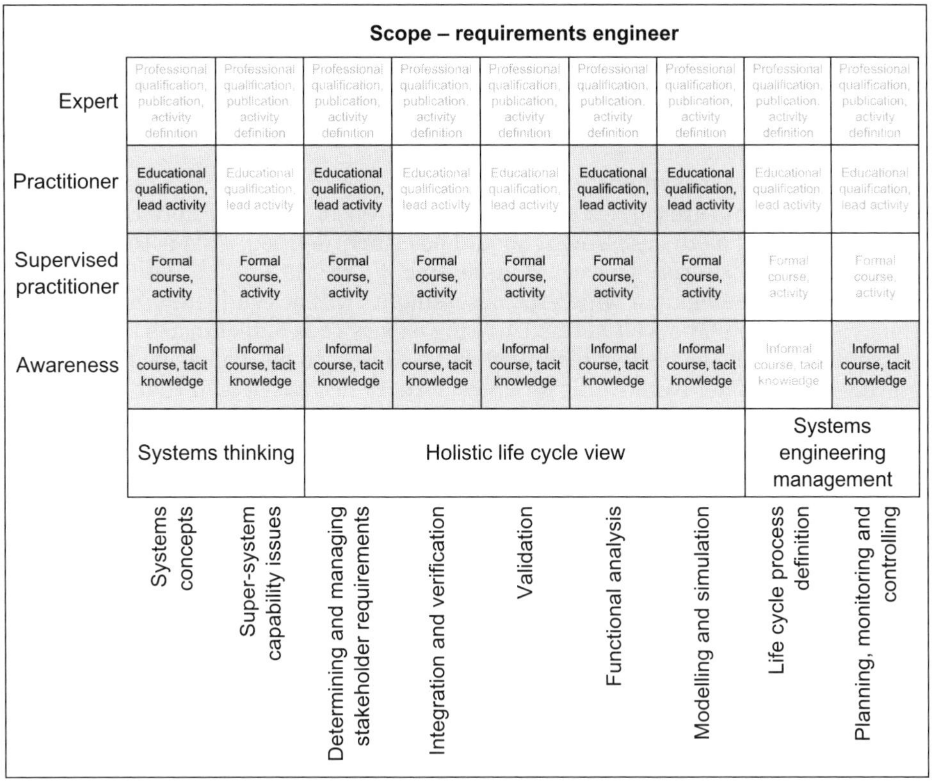

Figure 4.17 shows an example 'Competency Scope' for a requirements engineer role within an organisation. A number of competencies, grouped into competency area, are shown along the bottom of the diagram, here intended to show **all** the competencies from the organisation's 'Populated Applicable Competency Set'. The vertical axis indicates the various values of 'Level' that have been defined, with the contents of each cell defining the 'Evidence Type' for a given competency at a given level. The 'Competency Scope' itself is indicated by the shaded area. Thus, 'Validation' is to be assessed to 'Supervised practitioner' level only and 'Life-cycle process definition' is not to be assessed at all.

In practice, the number of competencies in a 'Populated Applicable Competency Set' is likely to be large and so all the competencies from the set are **not** all likely to be shown on a 'Competency Scope'. Also, all the competencies shown in Figure 4.17 are taken from the INCOSE Systems Engineering Competencies Framework but, as has been explained earlier, the whole point of the UCAM is that competencies from a number of different frameworks could, and in reality **would**, make up the 'Populated Applicable Competency Set' and any 'Competency Scope' generated from it.

Summary of the Assessment Set-up process

The 'Assessment Set-up' process exists to establish the 'Assessment Criteria' and 'Competency Scope(s)' for an assessment or set of assessments. The 'Competency Scope' is one of the main inputs to the 'Assessment' process, defining the competencies that will be assessed and the levels to which each will be assessed.

Discussion on the Assessment Set-up process

Not all assessments are carried out for the same reason and therefore the purpose (or purposes) of an assessment should be clearly defined. This is the role of the 'Assessment Criteria'. This set of 'Assessment Criteria' is what defines the 'Competency Scope' against which the assessments will be conducted. Such a competency scope should be well-defined, stating clearly the competencies that are to be assessed and the levels to which they will be assessed, as well as being practical in terms of assessment time and resources. Experience has shown that conducting an assessment with seven indicators to an average of level three can easily take up to three hours. When the preparation time and the time to analyse results is included, together with the fact that to conduct an assessment effectively requires two assessors (see the section on the 'Assessment' process below), this time can easily amount to a man-day of effort per assessment, so knowing the reasons for and scope of an assessment is vital in order to ensure that the time is well spent.

THE ASSESSMENT PROCESS

This section describes the 'Assessment' process introduced in 'The UCAM Processes' section above and executed in order to conduct an assessment.

Requirements for the Assessment process

The requirements for the 'Assessment' process are given below in Figure 4.18 which highlights the relevant requirements on the diagram introduced in Figure 4.1 above.

As can be seen in the diagram the main requirement for the 'Assessment' process is to 'Carry out assessment'. The activities that are needed in the process to meet this requirement, and the artefacts that form inputs to and outputs from the process are described in the following section.

Figure 4.18 Requirements for the Assessment process

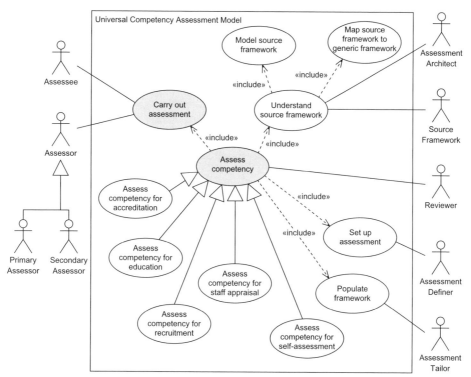

Contents of the Assessment process

The contents of the 'Assessment' process are shown in Figure 4.19, annotated to show whether the various artefacts are inputs or outputs (or both) from the process.

Figure 4.19 shows that there are nine activities that have to be carried out in the 'Assessment' process, namely 'assess indicator', 'calculate indicator set result', 'collate assessment information', 'determine competency profile', 'provide evidence', 'discuss assessment', 'select competency', 'select level' and 'update competency profile'. The process takes the 'Competency scope' output from the 'Assessment Set-up' process and uses it to generate the Competency profile(s) for the assessees, along with the other artefacts shown in Figure 4.19. The way that the 'Assessment Set-up' process is carried out is shown in the following section.

Figure 4.19 The contents of the Assessment process

«process»
Assessment
«out» Competency Profile «out» Evidence «inout» Record Sheet «out» Indicator Result «in» Rating Scheme «in» Competency Scope «out» Indicator Result Set
assess indicator calculate indicator set result collate assessment information determine competency profile provide evidence discuss assessment select competency select level update competency profile

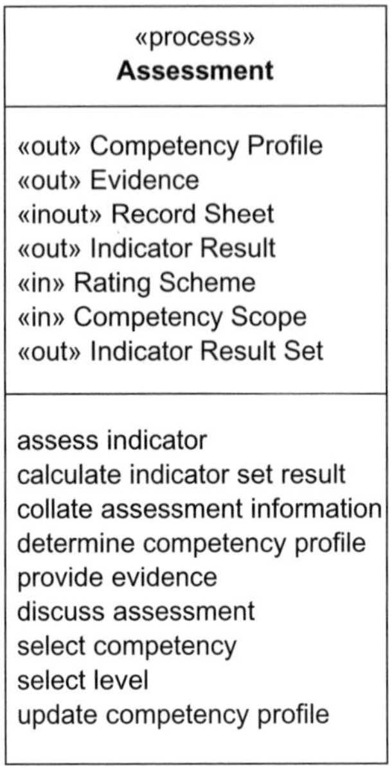

Carrying out the Assessment process

Figure 4.20 shows how the 'Assessment' process is carried out. The 'soft boxes' (rectangles with rounded corners) represent the various activities that have to be carried out and correspond with those shown in the bottom compartment in Figure 4.19. The vertical divisions (swim lanes) indicate which stakeholder role is responsible for carrying out which activity, and correspond to one or more of the stakeholder roles identified in Figure 4.2. The small rectangles containing arrows (known as 'pins') show inputs to and outputs from the various activities, with the name of the artefact flowing into or out of the activity shown on the line connecting the pins. These artefacts correspond to those found in the middle compartment in Figure 4.19.

The 'Assessment' process is carried out in order to perform an assessment based on a defined 'Competency Scope'. The output from the 'Assessment' process is a 'Competency Profile' showing the results of the assessment against the 'Competency Scope'.

Figure 4.20 shows that the 'Assessment' process begins with the 'Primary Assessor' executing the 'collate assessment information' activity. This is carried out to ensure that all the necessary information needed to carry out the assessment is available, such as the 'Competency Scope' against which the assessment is to be based and 'Record Sheet' on which the results of the assessment are to be recorded as the assessment proceeds. Once everything is ready, the 'Primary Assessor' executes the 'select competency' activity to choose the next competency to be assessed, followed by the 'select level' activity to choose the level to which the competency is to be assessed. These are based on information taken from the 'Competency Scope'.

Figure 4.20 Carrying out the Assessment process

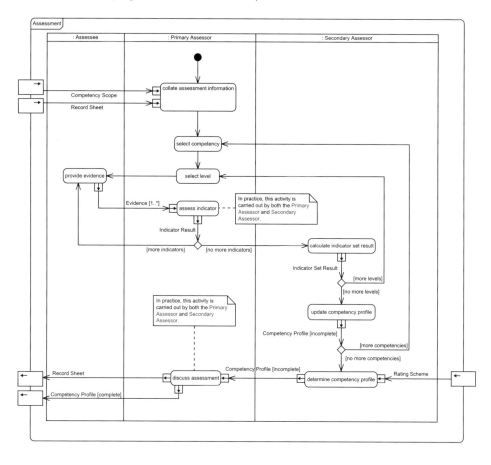

The 'Primary Assessor' then executes the 'assess indicator' activity during which he engages with the 'Assessee' in order to establish whether the 'Assessee' can present evidence to show that he has met the requirements of the indicator for the chosen competency and level. The 'Assessee' conducts the 'provide evidence' activity in order to present such evidence. The 'Primary Assessor' records a pass or fail for the indicator – the 'Indicator Result'. This activity is repeated for all the indicators of the selected competency-level combination.

When all the indicators have been covered, the 'Secondary Assessor' executes the 'calculate indicator set result' activity to convert the pass/fails to a simple percentage. For example, if a competency has five indicators at the chosen level and three are recorded as being passed and two as failed, then the 'Secondary Assessor' would calculate a percentage of 60 per cent for this competency level. This is the 'Indicator Set Result' for the competency and level.

If there are more levels to be assessed for the currently selected competency, then the process returns to 'select level' where it repeats for the next level. If all the levels for the selected competency have been covered, then the 'Secondary Assessor' executes the 'update competency profile' activity. This updates the incomplete 'Competency Profile' with the results for the selected competency, based on the 'Indicator Set Result' values for each level of assessment.

If there are more competencies to be assessed, as determined by the contents of the 'Competency Scope', then the process returns to the 'select competency' activity where it repeats for the next competency. If there are no more competencies to be assessed, then the 'Secondary Assessor' executes the 'determine competency scope' activity to produce a complete, but not yet finalised, 'Competency Profile'.

This 'Competency Profile' is discussed between the 'Primary Assessor' and 'Secondary Assessor' until agreement is reached on the proposed final, complete 'Competency Scope'. This gives both assessors the chance to discuss any issues that they may have with any of the results so that a 'Competency Scope' can be produced that they both are satisfied accurately reflects the outcome of the assessment. This 'Competency Scope' and the 'Record Sheet' used to capture the results during the assessment are the main outputs from the process.

It must be noted here that, of all the core UCAM processes, Figure 4.20 and the descriptive text above is the most 'theoretical' in that the diagram and text show an ordering of activities that, while they would work, would lead to a very stilted assessment being conducted. This is an inherent problem in trying to model something as flexible and often seemingly chaotic as human interaction. It must **never** be forgotten that the 'Assessment' process is meant to be carried out in as natural and non-threatening a manner as possible, something that it is almost impossible to capture easily in such a diagram.

Figures 4.19 and 4.20 show rather a large number of artefacts for the 'Assessment' process. The various artefacts of the process and their relationships are discussed further in the following section.

Artefacts of the Assessment process

The main output from the 'Assessment' process is the 'Competency Profile' for an assessee, generated based on the 'Competency Scope' and the results of the assessment. The artefacts of the 'Assessment' process, together with their relationships, are shown in Figure 4.21.

The 'Record Sheet' is used to record the results of the assessment by capturing each 'Indicator Result' for an 'Indicator' (basically a pass or fail along with a note of why), based on the 'Evidence' presented for the 'Indicator'. Each 'Indicator Result' for a given competency and level is grouped into an 'Indicator Result Set'. A piece of 'Evidence' must be one of the 'Evidence Type(s)' that is defined as being acceptable to demonstrate that an 'Indicator' has been met. The 'Record Sheet' will contain each 'Competency' and each associated 'Indicator' taken from the 'Competency Scope' that forms one of the main inputs to the 'Assessment' process. The 'Record Sheet' is represented in Figure 4.21 by the package in the middle of the diagram labelled, appropriately, 'Record Sheet'. A (very) small part of an example 'Record Sheet' is shown in Table 4.3.

Figure 4.21 Relationships between the artefacts of the Assessment process

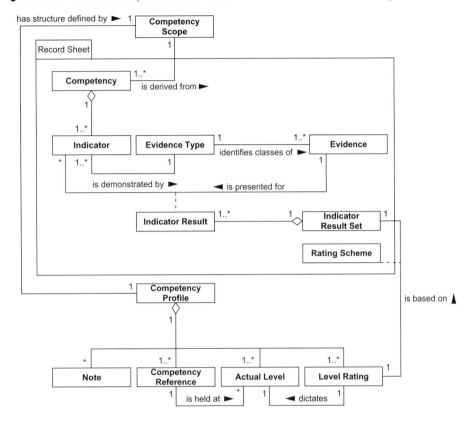

Table 4.3 shows the part of a completed 'Record Sheet' for a single competency and level (here, level 1 of the 'Systems concepts' competency). It shows each 'Indicator' for the competency, the acceptable 'Evidence Type' for each 'Indicator' and the actual 'Evidence' presented. A pass or fail result is noted for each 'Indicator' and a percentage calculated is based on these for the entire 'Indicator Set'. The 'Rating Scheme' in use is also shown, and the 'Level Rating' based on the percentage of 50 per cent is highlighted. Of course, the full 'Record Sheet' for an assessment will be much longer, containing similar information for each competency and level assessed.

The contents of the 'Record Sheet', along with the 'Competency Scope', are used to generate the 'Competency Profile' for the assessee, showing the 'Actual Level' at which each competency is held, together with any 'Note(s)' deemed relevant. An example 'Competency Profile' is shown in Figure 4.22.

Figure 4.22 shows an example 'Competency Profile' based on the 'Competency Scope' example shown earlier in Figure 4.22. This scope is shown on the diagram by the thick line that indicated the level to which each competency was assessed.

Table 4.3 Example of a completed 'Record Sheet' (partial) showing 'Rating Scheme'

Competency reference: 'System concepts', level 1				Rating scheme	
Indicator	**Evidence type**	**Evidence**	**Pass/ Fail**	**% range**	**Level rating**
Is aware of system life cycle	Informal course, tacit knowledge	Formal course certificate	Pass	81%–100%	Fully met
Is aware of hierarchy of systems	Informal course, tacit knowledge	No evidence	Fail	56%–80%	Largely met
Is aware of system context	Informal course, tacit knowledge	No evidence	Fail	**11%–55%**	**Partially met**
Is aware of interfaces	Informal course, tacit knowledge	Informal course certificate	Pass	0%–10%	Not met
		Rating %	**50%**		

For each competency and level that was assessed, the 'Level Rating' is shown in the corresponding cell. The 'Level Rating' is based on the 'Indicator Result Set' for the competency and level as determined by the 'Rating Scheme'. Thus, it can be seen that the assessee has 'Not met' the 'Validation' competency at any of the assessed levels, but has 'Fully met' the 'Modelling and simulation' at both 'Awareness' and 'Supervised practitioner' levels and has 'Partially met' it at 'Practitioner' level, the highest level to which it was assessed. Where a competency is 'Fully met', the cell has been shaded to emphasise the 'Actual Level' that has been reached for a competency and to make clearer the gaps, if there are any, between the 'Competency Profile' and the source 'Competency Scope'.

Summary of the Assessment process
The 'Assessment' process is executed to carry out an assessment. An assessment is carried out against a 'Competency Scope', with the results captured on a 'Record Sheet'. Using the defined 'Rating Scheme', these results are converted to a 'Competency Profile' for the assessee, showing how the assessee rates against the defined scope.

Discussion on the Assessment process
As noted above in the description of the 'Assessment' process, it is difficult to represent something as complex as human interaction on a simple diagram. It was also noted that any assessment should be carried out in as natural and

Figure 4.22 Example 'Competency Profile'

Competency profile								
Expert Not met	Not met	Not met	Not met	Not met	Not met	Not met	Not met	Not met
Practitioner Largely met	Not met	Partially met	Not met	Not met	Not met	Partially met	Not met	Not met
Supervised practitioner Partially met	Largely met	Fully met	Partially met	Not met	Partially met	Fully met	Not met	Partially met
Awareness Fully met	Fully met	Fully met	Fully met	Not met	Fully met	Fully met	Not met	Largely met
Systems thinking		Holistic life cycle view					Systems engineering management	
Systems concepts	Super-system capability issues	Determining and managing stakeholder requirements	Integration and verification	Validation	Functional analysis	Modelling and simulation	Life cycle process definition	Planning, monitoring and controlling

non-threatening a manner as possible. With this in mind, there are some points about the process that should be considered in order to help it run smoothly:

1. Experience has shown that attempting to carry out a competency assessment in a reasonable time and in a manner that ensures repeatability and as much objectivity as possible is very difficult with a single assessor. For this reason it is recommended that assessments are always carried out with both the primary and secondary assessor roles.

2. Assessors should always introduce themselves at the start of the process. The primary assessor should take the lead on this, and should explain to the assessee the reason for the assessment and the way in which the assessment will be carried out. The roles of the two assessors should be explained.

3. The primary assessor should concentrate on ensuring that the assessment flows in as smooth a manner as possible. In practice, the assessor will never be as mechanical in approach as suggested by the diagram in Figure 4.20, but will choose competencies and levels based on the responses of the assessee. The assessment should **not** simply be a list of questions on one indicator

after another, but should be as free-flowing and natural as possible (within the time set aside for the assessment). Doing this **and** recording results and capturing the evidence presented is almost impossible and this is why the secondary assessor is needed. The secondary assessor should concentrate on this recording of results but can also ask questions if it is felt that the primary assessor has missed any areas of the scope being assessed.

4. In order to ensure that the assessment is as free-flowing as possible, it is essential that both the primary and secondary assessors are familiar with the competency frameworks being used as the basis of assessment, and also, if possible, with the domain areas being covered by the assessment. In this way, they are not constantly having to look through and read the scope or other information on the competencies in order to understand what they are assessing and can also understand the responses given by the assessee when determining the pass or fail for a given indicator. At the very least, it is recommended that the primary assessor be familiar with the domain being covered by the assessment. To this end, examples of competency profiles for the assessor roles are provided later in this chapter.

5. At the end of the assessment the primary assessor should explain to the assessee what happens next. In practice, it has been found that the assessee should leave the room once all the competencies and levels have been covered. The 'determine competency profile' and 'discuss assessment' activities in Figure 4.20 should not be conducted with the assessee present. In addition, the 'determine competency profile' activity might actually be carried out after the assessment. This is certainly the most effective method where a large number of assessments have to be made. It is often better to leave the assessment with an agreed 'Record Sheet' for the assessee and determine the profile later. Whether the 'Record Sheet' is made available to the assessee is something that should be decided prior to conducting the assessment, but in the authors' experience it is better not to include this with the 'Competency Profile' that **is** given to the assessee.

For a competency assessment to be successful, the competency of assessors has to be ensured in terms of their domain knowledge of both the industry in which assessees work and in terms of the frameworks that are being used for the assessment. There should always be **at least** two assessors to ensure that the assessment flows smoothly and assessors should ensure that the assessment is non-intimidating and non-threatening. It should be a conversation and discussion with the assessee and **not** an interrogation that simply works through a checklist of questions.

Assessments can take an unexpected amount of time to conduct, even excluding any pre-assessment preparation on the part of the assessees (and assessors). As was noted previously, experience has shown that to assess against seven competencies to an average of level three typically takes around three hours. It is therefore essential that sufficient time is allocated for an assessment and that the competency scopes used are practical. If the assessees have some familiarity with the contents of the framework prior to an assessment, this can help ensure that it runs in a timely fashion. Having all supporting evidence to hand also makes the assessors' roles easier when it comes to deciding whether the necessary evidence has been presented to support a competency.

Finally, it should be explained to assessees that competency levels may go down as well as up. This is **not** a bad thing but simply reflects the changes in competencies as an assessee's career progresses and roles change. Someone working in the software industry who previously spent all day developing software in a particular programming language would be expected to be a 'practitioner' (if not even an 'expert') in appropriate competencies relating to that language and associated techniques. If, five years later, that same person is now managing a software project, and hasn't developed software using that language for a number of years, then their level of competency will have dropped (although it could probably be quickly brought back up to the previous level if they again had to actively develop software). This doesn't mean that they have now become incompetent; just that their roles have changed. They will hold other competencies at higher levels than they did previously and are even likely to hold completely different competencies reflecting their new roles. Of course, if competencies drop over time for an assessee whose role has **not** changed, then this is an indication of a problem with their competency to do their job.

UCAM SUPPORT PROCESSES

The four processes discussed in the previous sections form the **core** processes of UCAM and are executed to ensure that the competency assessment elements described in the UCAM meta-model (see Chapter 3) are created and utilised. As shown in Figure 4.3 above and previously discussed, there are a number of UCAM support processes that can be carried out prior to and following execution of the core UCAM processes.

When tailoring UCAM for use within an organisation, a large part of the tailoring effort is likely to be needed in the identification and definition of these non-core UCAM **support** processes. These support processes can be organised into two groups: the pre-assessment processes that are executed before the core UCAM processes and the post-assessment processes that are run afterwards.

In this section a number of possible support processes are discussed. This is not meant to be an exhaustive definition, but is intended to give an indication of the types of support process that will be needed when tailoring UCAM. Also, it is not the intention here to define these processes in detail, since the exact nature of each process will depend on the requirements of the tailoring organisation. For each process introduced, a simple text description will be provided. The pre-assessment processes are introduced first and are shown in Figure 4.23.

Figure 4.23 identifies four types of 'Pre-assessment Process', which are discussed below. Note the use of the '{incomplete}' constraint to show that not every possible 'Pre-assessment Process' has been identified. The processes shown are:

Figure 4.23 The Pre-assessment Processes

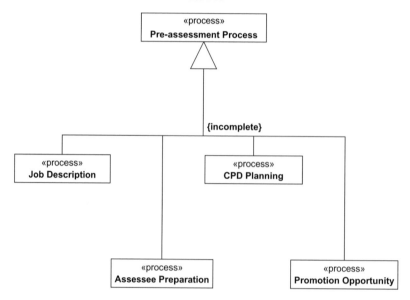

1. 'Job Description'. This process would be executed when UCAM is to be used to support recruitment. The 'Job Description' process is responsible for identifying the competencies necessary for a given job, perhaps helping to identify source frameworks that could be used as a basis of recruitment assessment or identifying relevant competencies from frameworks that have already been selected. In this way the outputs from the 'Job Description' process could feed into the core 'Framework Population' process to help define competency scopes or even applicable competency sets.

2. 'Assessee Preparation'. This process is responsible for informing assessees of the purpose and scope of an assessment and of the types of evidence that will be required. The assessees can then gather such evidence and even familiarise themselves with the framework(s) against which they will be assessed. This may or may not be desirable, as knowledge of the content of an assessment framework often leads some assessees to study the framework in an attempt to 'beat the system'. This process would normally be executed prior to the core 'Assessment' process.

3. 'CPD Planning'. This process would be executed when UCAM is to be used for self-assessment as part of a CPD activity. The process is intended to force assessees into considering which CPD aspects are to be assessed and hence to help identify any source frameworks or competencies that are needed for the assessment. It could therefore feed into the core 'Framework Definition' or 'Framework Population' processes.

4. 'Promotion Opportunity'. This process is intended to support those who want to apply for a promotion. It would lead them through a gap analysis to identify the differences in the competencies that they currently hold, and the

levels at which they are held, as against the required competencies and levels for the new position. As with the 'CPD Planning' process, it would then help to identify any source frameworks for missing competencies. For competencies that they hold at a lower level than is required, the process would help to identify any indicators that must be demonstrated to gain the competency at the higher level.

The post-assessment processes are shown in Figure 4.24, which identifies five types of 'Post-assessment Process'. Again, note the use of the '{incomplete}' constraint to show that not every possible 'Post-assessment Process' has been identified. Also, although the diagram shows six types of 'Post-assessment Process', one of them (the 'Training Analysis' process) is shown as being {Abstract}. This means that although 'Training Analysis' is a meaningful concept for a type of process, it cannot exist in its own right but identifies a type of process that requires a **concrete** 'Training Analysis' process (such as 'Trainer Assessment') to implement it. (To understand the concept, think about the concepts of 'mammal' and 'cat'. Mammal is a meaningful concept but is abstract in that there is no such thing as a 'mammal'. You cannot go to a zoo and see a creature that is just a mammal, but you can see **types** of mammals such as cats.)

Figure 4.24 The Post-assessment Processes

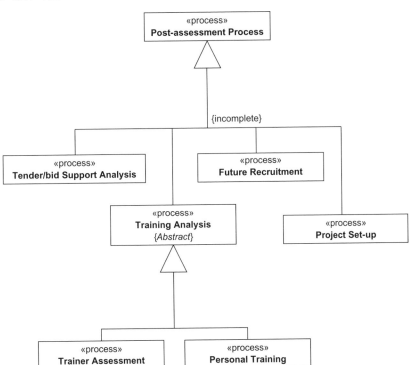

The processes shown are:

1. 'Tender/bid Support Analysis'. Traditionally, when responding to tenders for work, organisations have supplied CVs (**résumés**) for the staff members that they intend to use on the project in order to support their tender responses. CVs are, however, largely subjective in what they say about their subject and many organisations issuing tenders for work are now requiring that more objective information be provided about the competence of any person put forward for the project. This process is intended to be used by an organisation responding to a tender. It covers the analysis of a tender in order to determine the competencies that will be required by the people being put forward to work on the project that is the subject of the tender. It then covers the identification of the staff who have the required competencies, so that their details can be included in the tender response.

2. 'Trainer Assessment'. This process is used to identify training requirements from a trainer's point of view. It takes the results of an assessment (or set of assessments) and uses them to help a trainer understand the areas in which people require competence. This can then be used to help drive the creation of new courses and the tailoring of existing courses towards delivering these competencies.

3. 'Personal Training'. This process takes the results of an assessment and uses them to perform a personal training needs analysis, based on the competency profile generated by the assessment, in order to bring competencies up to the levels defined in the competency profile. If required, the process can also cover the arrangement of such training and participation in the training.

4. 'Future Recruitment'. This process is executed in order to determine future recruitment needs for an organisation (or part of an organisation). By looking at the existing **combined** competency profile of an organisation (created by combining the competency profiles of all individuals in the organisation) and comparing it against a competency scope created to identify future **organisational** competency needs, then it is possible to identify organisational competency gaps. This gap analysis can then be used to drive future recruitment by feeding into the 'Job Description' **pre**-assessment process when UCAM-based assessments are used as part of the future recruitment activity.

5. 'Project Set-up'. Getting the balance of competencies right for a project team is a necessary (although not sufficient) condition for project success. This process defines a competency scope not for an individual or a role but for a project and then takes the competency profiles of candidate team members and compares them against each other and against this scope. The aim is to ensure that the required competencies for the project are met by the sum of the competencies of each individual. In effect, the process ensures that a combined competency profile for the candidate team members (hopefully) matches or exceeds the competency scope for the project. Where there are gaps between the required and actual competencies, the process helps to pick the best match. The 'Personal Training' or 'Future Recruitment' processes could then be executed to close any such gaps.

Examples of using some of these UCAM support processes are given in the following section, which discusses scenarios for using UCAM.

USING UCAM

The UCAM may be used to carry out competency assessments for a variety of reasons. In each case, although the four core UCAM processes will always be needed, the order in which they are executed and, indeed, the number of times each one is executed may vary. Each reason for carrying out a competency assessment may be thought of as a different **scenario** for the application of the UCAM. This section briefly discusses three such scenarios and shows how the processes to be used and the order in which they are executed can be documented. It should be stressed that these scenarios show a few possible examples and do not, as such, represent an exhaustive list of possibilities.

Using UCAM for self-assessment

A common use for competency assessments is to undertake self-assessment, perhaps in order to establish personal training needs, as represented by the 'Assess competency for self-assessment' requirement in Figure 4.1 above. One such scenario is shown in Figure 4.25.

Figure 4.25 Scenario showing process execution for self-assessment

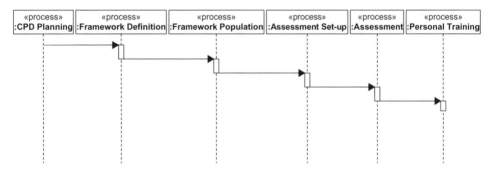

Figure 4.25 shows that in order to assess personal training needs for CPD, it is first necessary to execute the 'CPD Planning' process. This is one of the pre-UCAM support processes discussed above and is used here to establish which CPD aspects are to be assessed and hence to help identify any source frameworks that are needed for the assessment. The four core UCAM processes are then run in the order 'Framework Definition', 'Framework Population', 'Assessment Set-up' and 'Assessment' so as to understand any frameworks against which the self-assessment is to take place, set-up and then carry out the self-assessment.

Once the assessment is complete, it is necessary to use the results of the assessment to determine and then conduct the training that is required. The post-UCAM 'Personal Training' process is responsible for this aspect of the scenario.

Note here that the first such self-assessment exercise may be quite time-consuming due to the amount of work typically required by the 'Framework Definition' and 'Framework Population' processes. However, subsequent self-assessments should be much quicker as, although these two processes should still be executed, they should only take significant time if the source frameworks or applicable competency sets have changed. Such changes to the frameworks and applicable competency sets will typically be needed for self-assessments that are undertaken after a change of job role or responsibility. Also, if the organisation has already modelled the relevant competency frameworks, and so on, then the self-assessment burden is reduced.

Using UCAM for recruitment

The UCAM requirements shown in Figure 4.1 include the requirement to be able to 'Assess competency for recruitment'. When using UCAM for this purpose, a typical scenario is shown in Figure 4.26.

Figure 4.26 Scenario showing process execution for recruitment

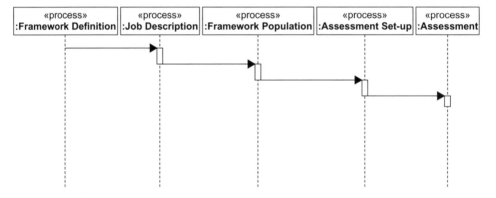

The scenario shows that in order to use the UCAM for recruitment, the first process that should be run is the 'Framework Definition' process. This ensures that the framework's defining competencies that are relevant to the work undertaken by the organisation are clearly understood. The pre-UCAM 'Job Description' process is then executed, taking the framework information and information on the job to produce a job description described in terms of the competencies contained in the source frameworks. These competencies and the job description then feed into the 'Framework Population' process in order to help establish the applicable competency set and evidence types that are needed in order to carry out competency assessments as part of the recruitment process. The 'Assessment Set-up' and 'Assessment' processes are carried out in order to undertake the assessments, with the job description helping to define the competency scope as part of the 'Assessment Set-up' process.

Again, as with using UCAM for self-assessment, the first time it is used is likely to be time-consuming due to the nature of the 'Framework Definition' and 'Framework Population' processes. However, the time required will reduce with subsequent uses of the processes for recruitment as more and more frameworks are captured and the applicable competency sets, evidence types and even competency scopes are developed and enlarged with continued use.

Using UCAM for appraisals

When using the UCAM processes to meet the requirement to 'Assess competency for staff appraisal', then the scenario in Figure 4.27 applies.

Figure 4.27 Scenario showing process execution for appraisals

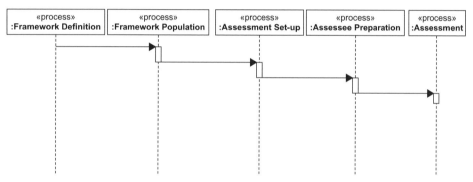

When using UCAM to conduct staff appraisals, it is first necessary to ensure that any source frameworks are understood, competencies identified and evidence types defined. The 'Framework Definition' and 'Framework Population' processes are run first to ensure that this preparation is carried out. The 'Assessment Set-up' process is then executed to define the various competency scopes that will be used as the basis of the assessments. The pre-UCAM 'Assessee Preparation' process is then executed. This informs the assessees of the purpose and scope of the assessment and of the types of evidence that will be required. The assessees can then gather such evidence and even familiarise themselves with the framework(s) against which they will be assessed. Once all are ready, the 'Assessment' process is executed in order to carry out the assessments.

This scenario describes what is, perhaps, the most common use of competency assessment. As with the other scenarios described above, repeated use of the UCAM processes will require less time as competency frameworks are understood and the supporting information such as applicable competency sets, evidence types and competency scopes are defined and reused from assessment to assessment.

Scenarios for the remaining two requirements of 'Assess competency for accreditation' and 'Assess competency for education' are not given here. Their definition is left as an exercise for the reader.

COMPETENCY OF ASSESSORS

It is essential that the assessors who carry out the assessments are competent to do the job. It would be irony indeed if this were not the case. However, the fact that this section even exists indicates that this is sometimes the case.

This section shows example competency profiles for the roles of primary and secondary assessor and also provides some guidelines for readers to define their own profiles for assessors. The profile for the primary assessor is considered first. This is followed by an example profile for the secondary assessor.

A key point that must be emphasised here is that this section shows competency **profiles** rather than competency **scopes**. This is essential. A competency scope shows the **desired** competencies and levels against which someone is assessed, whereas a competency profile shows the **actual** competencies and levels that someone has attained. For the primary and secondary assessors, it is the actual competencies and levels that need to be defined and not the desired competencies – hence the need for competency profiles rather than competency scopes. It is also important to note that the profiles shown are the **minimum** needed.

The competency profile in Figure 4.28 is an example of the required profile for a primary assessor who will be carrying out a competency assessment against the competency scope shown earlier in Figure 4.17. The first thing to notice is that this profile includes some additional competencies not found in Figure 4.17, namely 'Communicate in English with Others at All Levels' and 'Demonstrate Personal and Social Skills'. These are competencies from the 'Demonstrate Interpersonal Skills' competency theme from the UKSPEC framework and reflect the fact that the primary assessor must be able to talk with assessees, no matter what their level. The other competencies shown are from the INCOSE Systems Engineering Competencies Framework, illustrating one of the key concepts of the UCAM approach – the ability to mix competencies from different frameworks. The source frameworks are shown on the profile for clarity.

The two 'Demonstrate Interpersonal Skills' competencies, along with the two 'Systems thinking' competencies are here considered to be absolutely fundamental competencies that the primary assessor must hold at 'Practitioner' level. They are competencies that the primary assessor **must** actively and regularly undertake as a practitioner, since they are fundamental to being able to interact with assessees in order to conduct an assessment and to having sufficient understanding of the principles behind systems thinking. All the other competencies need only be held at 'Supervised practitioner' level. The primary assessor needs to be sufficiently versed in these areas to be able to carry out work in them, but this can be work that can be carried out under supervision. When carrying out an assessment, the

Figure 4.28 Example Primary Assessor Competency Profile

	Communicate in English with others at all levels	Demonstrate personal and social skills	Systems concepts	Super-system capability issues	Determining and managing stakeholder requirements	Integration and verification	Validation	Functional analysis	Modelling and simulation	Life cycle process definition	Planning, monitoring and controlling
Scope – Primary Assessor											
Expert											
Practitioner	Fully met	Fully met	Fully met	Fully met							
Supervised practitioner	Fully met	Fully met	Fully met	Fully met	Fully met	Fully met	Fully met	Fully met	Fully met		Fully met
Awareness	Fully met	Fully met	Fully met	Fully met	Fully met	Fully met	Fully met	Fully met	Fully met		Fully met
	UKSPEC		INCOSE Systems Engineering Competencies Framework								
	Demonstrate interpersonal skills		Systems thinking		Holistic life cycle view					Systems engineering management	

primary assessor needs to be able to understand what is being said by the assessee and to ask the necessary questions to conduct the assessment. In general, this does not require that the primary assessor be at the same level in a particular competency as the assessee. For example, it is possible for a primary assessor to judge that an assessee is an expert in a particular competency without being an expert himself.

An example competency profile for the secondary assessor is given in Figure 4.29. This, importantly, assumes that the profile is based on the same scope as that used for the definition of the primary assessor's profile.

As can be seen in Figure 4.29, the competencies for the secondary assessor are the same as those for the primary assessor. However, it can also be seen that all the levels are one lower than for the primary assessor. This reflects the role that the secondary assessor plays in an assessment, which is largely that of a recorder of evidence and creator of competency profiles. In order to record correctly an assessee's responses, the secondary assessor needs a certain level of understanding of what is being said. Similarly, in order to prompt the primary assessor if any competencies have been missed, the secondary assessor must have an understanding of what has and has not been covered. However, this level of knowledge need not be as high as that required by the primary assessor; hence the secondary assessor should have at least 'Supervised practitioner' level in the fundamental competencies and 'Awareness' level in the rest.

Figure 4.29 Example Secondary Assessor Competency Profile

	Scope – Secondary Assessor											
Expert												
Practitioner												
Supervised practitioner	Fully met	Fully met	Fully met	Fully met								
Awareness	Fully met	Fully met	Fully met	Fully met	Fully met	Fully met	Fully met	Fully met	Fully met		Fully met
	UKSPEC		**INCOSE Systems Engineering Competencies Framework**									
	Demonstrate interpersonal skills		Systems thinking		Holistic life cycle view						Systems engineering management	
	Communicate in English with others at all levels	Demonstrate personal and social skills	Systems concepts	Super-system capability issues	Determining and managing stakeholder requirements	Integration and verification	Validation	Functional analysis	Modelling and simulation	Life cycle process definition	Planning, monitoring and controlling

From the above discussion, there are a number of points that need to be considered when defining the competency profiles for a primary and secondary assessor:

1. Primary and secondary assessor profiles must be defined based on a particular competency scope (or scopes) for the assessment that the assessors are to carry out.

2. A primary assessor does **not** need to be a practitioner (or even an expert) in all the competencies to be assessed. There are a number of fundamental competencies that **must** be held at practitioner level, but it is usually sufficient for the other competencies to be held at supervised practitioner level.

3. The two 'Demonstrate Interpersonal Skills' competencies taken from UKSPEC (or similar competencies from other frameworks) will **always** be two of the fundamental competencies that a primary assessor must hold at practitioner level. The other fundamental competencies will depend on the scope of the competency assessment.

4. The secondary assessor should have a profile containing the same competencies as the primary assessor, but these competencies can be held at one level lower than for the primary assessor.

5. Although not shown in the competency profiles above, it is assumed that both the primary and secondary assessors are familiar with the concepts and content of whatever approach, such as UCAM, that is being used to carry out the assessments. Relevant competencies in the approach should be considered as belonging to the fundamental competencies needed by the assessors and therefore should be held at 'Practitioner' level by the primary assessor and 'Supervised practitioner' by the secondary assessor, as a minimum.

6. Given that a primary assessor will need to hold certain competencies based on the competency scope of the assessment to be carried out, this means that primary assessors will need to be matched to the assessments that they will be conducting. A person cannot simply be assigned to the primary assessor role to carry out any assessment. They must be assigned based on how their competency profile matches that of the primary assessor profile for the assessment. The same may also be true of secondary assessors, but given that the levels required for competencies are lower than for a primary assessor, there is likely to be greater flexibility when assigning people to the secondary assessor role.

This section has presented example competency profiles for both the primary and secondary assessor roles. Remember, however, that these profiles were necessarily based on a defined competency scope for a particular assessment and that this will always be the case. It is not sufficient to ask someone to perform one of the assessor roles simply because they have taken that role in an assessment in the past. If they do not hold the necessary competencies at the required levels for the scope of the assessment they are being asked to assess, they are unlikely to be able to carry out the assessment in a professional, competent manner.

CONCLUSIONS

Many competency frameworks exist that can be used as the source of competencies for an organisation to use when carrying out competency assessments. In order to understand these frameworks, decide on the competencies that are relevant to an organisation and help to ensure repeatable and measurable competency assessments, as a defined approach to the understanding of candidate framework and the set-up and carrying out of assessments is needed.

Unfortunately most, if not all, competency frameworks neglect this aspect of competency assessment. The UCAM, a model and process-based approach to competency assessments is one possible solution. This chapter has described the set of four **core** processes that make up the UCAM and are aimed at addressing these aspects. Additional non-core **support** processes have also been discussed. These support process are typically executed before or after the core UCAM processes in order to help with, for example, the set-up or analysis of assessments.

REFERENCES

Holt, J. (2009) *A pragmatic guide to business process modelling,* second edition. BCS, the Chartered Institute for IT, Swindon.

Holt, J. and Perry, S. (2008) *SysML for systems engineering.* IET Publishing, Herts, UK.

5   CASE STUDIES

Gissa job
Yosser Hughes

INTRODUCTION

This chapter looks at real-life case studies where the ideas and approach introduced in this book have been put into practice. There are three case studies: one concerned with creating a new competency framework for a specific organisation, one focusing on assessing against an established framework, and one that looks at a combination of the two.

CASE STUDY 1 – GENERATING A NEW FRAMEWORK

Introduction to case study

This case study is concerned with a small engineering consultancy company. The company has fewer than 50 employees but prides itself on the ability and reputation of its staff. The first step with any piece of work is to understand why the work is required, and generating a competency framework is no exception. There were many good reasons why the competency framework was required, which included the following:

- Due to the nature of the core business – consultancy work – the competence of individual staff members is seen as being the major selling point of the company. Therefore, any mechanism that promotes their abilities is seen as a very good thing.

- Competition is always a threat to any business and the CEO of the company was frustrated that many of their alleged competitors were putting forward vastly inferior personnel for the same projects. After all, it costs nothing to name a person as a 'consultant', but how do you prove the pedigree of any consultant?

- An essential part of the company ethos is to be leading the field in all areas; therefore, by being early-adopters of a competency-based approach, this was seen as fulfilling a key business requirement.

These were the business reasons why the work was seen to be important, which then led onto considering what, exactly, would need to be done to fulfil these business reasons. These requirements for the work were identified as follows:

- Generate profiles for all relevant stakeholders. All key consultants in the business take on a number of stakeholder roles, and it was decided, in line with best practice, to define competency scopes from which the competency profiles would be generated based on these roles. This is important, as different job titles can take on many different roles, so defining scopes for each job title, as opposed to for a set of roles, was seen as being incorrect.

- Identify sources standards. A large part of the business is to be driven by and is to promote best practice in all its forms, including using established standards. Therefore, one of the key drivers for this work was to use internationally recognised source standards that could be used as a start point for the competency work. Where a framework was deemed not to be quite appropriate, then a bespoke framework would be defined that maps back to, and complies with, the source standards.

- Identify relevant competencies. Based on the source standards, a set of relevant competencies would be identified. It was anticipated that some of these would be at quite a high level and, therefore, new competencies would be defined in the bespoke framework. These new competencies would, of course, map back to the core competencies identified in the source standards.

- Set levels. For each of the competencies, it was decided that the level would be set based on the stakeholder role. For the bespoke framework, the number of levels defined would again be compatible with the source frameworks.

With these points in mind, it was decided to carry out the work in accordance with the UCAM processes. This section focuses on the generation of the bespoke framework, rather than carrying out the assessments themselves (discussed elsewhere in this chapter), so the main processes that will be discussed are: framework definition and framework population.

Framework definition process

The first of the UCAM processes that was executed was the 'Framework Definition' process. This was executed in order to generate a new competency framework. Therefore, as well as understanding the source framework (covered elsewhere) this is the process where the framework for the bespoke application was defined.

Figure 5.1 shows the basic elements in the framework that were defined for the company. This was generated based on the internal structure of the company, but also bearing in mind which of the source frameworks would be used (in this case, the INCOSE competencies framework).

The framework in Figure 5.1 shows that the 'Company Competency Framework' maps onto one or more 'Competency Framework(s)'. This represents the various standard frameworks that were used as sources in this work. In this application, one of the main frameworks was the INCOSE competencies framework with additional competencies taken from those in SFIA.

The structure is such that the 'Company Competency Framework' is made up of three 'Competency Type(s)', each of which is made up of one or more 'Competency Area(s)', each of which is made up of one or more 'Competency(ies)', each of which is made up of one or more 'Indicator(s)'. This is a basic structural hierarchy that has a clean mapping onto UCAM – as will be shown in Table 5.1.

Figure 5.1 Structure of the competency framework

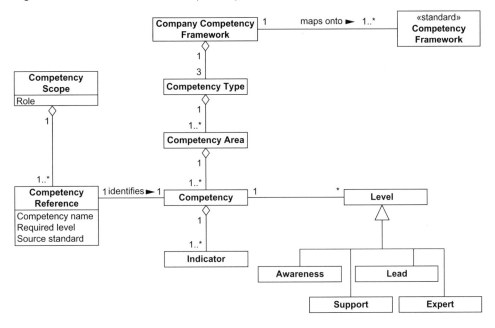

Each 'Competency' is held at a single 'Level', and there are four levels: 'Awareness', 'Support', 'Lead' and 'Expert'. The definition of these levels is very important and will be discussed in some detail in the next section. This framework also has the concept of a 'Competency Scope' that is made up of one or more 'Competency Reference(s)', each of which references a single 'Competency'. The Table 5.1 shows the definitions, as specified in the company's enterprise architecture, and their mapping back to the UCAM terminology.

Table 5.1 Basic definitions and mapping to UCAM

Term	Definition	UCAM reference
Competency Type	This is the generic classification of competencies at the highest level	No direct mapping, as this is a higher-level categorisation of Competency Areas
Systems Knowledge	A type of 'Competency Type' (not shown in the diagram), that describes the generic, cross-cutting competencies required.	Technical

(Continued)

Table 5.1 *(Continued)*

Term	Definition	UCAM reference
Skill	A type of 'Competency Type' (not shown in the diagram), that describes the technique and notation-specific competencies required	Skill
Domain Knowledge	A type of 'Competency Type' (not shown in the diagram), that describes the domain-specific competencies required	Domain Knowledge
Competency Area	The basic categorisation of competencies	Competency Area
Competency	The actual competencies to be assessed	Competency
Indicator	Each competency is defined in terms of a number of indicators, which are the things that are actually assessed during an assessment	Indicator
Level	This represents the level at which each competency may be held. In the company model, there are four levels defined: awareness, support, lead and expert	Level
Awareness	This level describes the ability to speak knowledgeably about a particular aspect of the competency. The main aim is for the assessee to demonstrate that they understand each indicator fully, and back this up with examples – either theoretical or real-life	Type of 'Level'
Support	This level reflects the ability to implement the concepts that were discussed at level 1 for this competency	Type of 'Level'
Lead	This level reflects the ability to be able to lead the activity that was described at level 1 and implemented at level 2. Level 3, Lead, is the minimum requirement for a member of staff to be able to be considered as a consultant for the related competency	Type of 'Level'
Expert	This level reflects the ability to be a true, recognised expert in the field that is described by this competency	Type of 'Level'

(Continued)

Table 5.1 *(Continued)*

Term	Definition	UCAM reference
Competency Scope	The set of competencies from the sources that is specific to this organisation	Applicable Competency Set
Competency Reference	A reference to an actual competency	Competency Reference

Table 5.1 shows the definitions of the basic terms and the mapping to UCAM, but this is really only the tip of the iceberg. To simply come up with definitions and map them is relatively simple, but what is far more difficult is coming up with a scheme that is realistic and that adds value to the whole assessment process.

During the framework definition process, it was decided to use the INCOSE competencies framework for the basis of the company framework, but it was felt that, after investigation, the system employed in the INCOSE framework was not workable for this particular company. In particular, a few issues were raised:

- The number of indicators for the various competencies was not consistent. For example, some competencies, such as 'Maintain Design Integrity' at 'Awareness' level had only a single indicator, whereas others, such as 'Determining and Managing Stakeholder Requirements' at 'Practitioner' level, had 18 indicators. It was decided that the basic number of indicators should have a more consistent nature, therefore, the way that indicators work was to be changed. It was decided that the 'seven plus or minus two' rule would be applied to the number of indicators to give this consistency.

- The INCOSE framework has different indicators identified at different levels, which makes the whole assessment process more complex and there is a lot more 'paper shuffling' involved, as there is a different set of competencies defined not only for each competency (to be expected) but also at each level. It was decided that a simpler approach would be required.

Bearing these issues in mind, it was decided to look at other approaches to assessments and to see if anything could be learned from them. One obvious candidate for assessment knowledge is the world of capability assessment which, as discussed previously in this book, is very closely related to competency assessment. Two of the main approaches to assessment that were looked at were the CMMI (see CMMI) and SPICE (see SPICE). In each of these assessment approaches, the indicators that describe individual processes are defined at level 1 only, and then the indicators for each of the other levels (levels 2 to 5 in both cases) are generic indicators that are the same for every process. In this way, the description of the process is contained in the indicators at level 1. The indicators for all other levels are defined as the same for each level – in reality, each indicator will have a set of questions associated with it, which means that the same set of questions can be asked at levels 2 to 4. By approaching the assessment in this manner, it makes the assessment far simpler from an assessor's point of view, as it is far easier to learn the generic indicators at each level and, therefore, run a far more fluid assessment. This concept is more clearly illustrated by looking at how it was applied in this particular case study.

The competencies

This part of the case study looks at defining two types of competency:

- 'Systems Knowledge' competencies, which are based on the ones defined in the source INCOSE framework. These competencies represent generic concepts that may be applied across various parts of an organisation as systems engineering enablers, and do not identify any specific techniques;

- 'Skill' competencies, which are specific implementations of the generic systems knowledge competencies. These skills describe specific techniques, such as particular modelling languages (for example, UML, SysML), particular processes (for example, UCAM, seven views), and so on.

The 'System Knowledge' competency that was taken as the start point was the 'Modelling and Simulation' competency from the INCOSE framework. One of the main business activities of the company is the application of modelling; therefore, it was deemed that the INCOSE definition of modelling was not appropriate for this particular business. As a result of this, it was decided to redefine the basic modelling competency. This is perfectly acceptable as the INCOSE framework, as with any of these source frameworks, is only there for guidance rather than being a strict authority on the content of a competency framework.

Figure 5.2 shows how the new competencies were defined.

Figure 5.2 The Systems Knowledge competency type

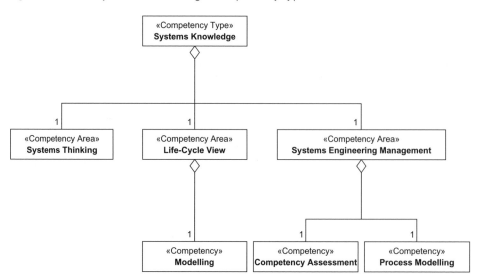

Figure 5.2 shows that the 'Systems Knowledge' competency type is made up of:

- the 'Systems Thinking' competency area, which has no competencies;
- the 'Life-cycle View' competency area, which has a 'Modelling' competency defined;
- the 'Systems Engineering Management' competency area, which has two competencies identified, which are: 'Competency Assessment' and 'Process Modelling'.

In reality, each of the competencies in the above list actually had more competencies defined, but they are not shown here for the sake of brevity. For each of these competencies, a number of indicators were defined that describe the core elements that characterise each competency. These are described in Table 5.2.

Table 5.2 Definition of level 1 indicators for 'Systems Knowledge' competencies

Competency	Description	Indicators
Modelling	This competency relates to generic modelling.	<ul><li>Understands the need for modelling</li><li>Can provide an appropriate definition of modelling</li><li>Understands the concept of abstraction</li><li>Understands the concept of connection to reality</li><li>Understands the concept of different approaches to modelling</li><li>Understands the concept of consistency</li><li>Can define what a view is</li><li>Understands the difference between modelling and drawing pictures</li><li>Understands structural modelling</li><li>Understands behavioural modelling</li></ul>
Process Modelling	This competency reflects the ability to model processes	<ul><li>Understands the need for process</li><li>Understands what a stakeholder is</li><li>Understands the drivers behind process modelling (complexity, communication, lack of understanding)</li><li>Can define what a process is, in terms of activities, artefacts and stakeholders</li><li>Is aware of different approaches or techniques to process modelling</li><li>Is aware of the importance of views</li><li>Understands how a good process model may be used (assessment, audits, process improvement, and so on)</li></ul>

(Continued)

Table 5.2 *(Continued)*

Competency	Description	Indicators
Competency Assessment	This competency reflects the understanding of the concept of competency assessment.	• Understands the need for competency assessment • Understands the specific drivers behind why someone may wish to perform a competency assessment • Can define competency • Understands the difference between capability and competency • Understands the concept of competency groups or areas • Understands what indicators are • Understands what a competency level is • Can provide examples of how the output of an assessment may be used

The next part of this case study will be the idea of the 'Skill', which has been defined as 'Competency Type'. This is chosen as it shows how competencies can be created from scratch, rather than tailoring what is already there. Figure 5.3 shows the skills that have been identified.

Figure 5.3 shows that the 'Skill' competency type is made up of 'Technical Skill', which is itself a competency area. It should be noted that there is more than one competency area for this competency type, but only one is shown here, for the sake of brevity. The 'Technical Skill' competency area is made up of a number of competencies, which are: 'UML Modelling', 'SysML Modelling', 'Use Case Modelling', 'Seven Views Approach' and 'UCAM Assessment'. Each of these competencies represents a very specific technique or approach to performing modelling, which is why they are skills, rather than being represented by the generic 'Modelling and Simulation' competency defined in the source INCOSE framework, or the 'Modelling' competency area discussed previously.

Also shown in Figure 5.3 is the concept of the 'Soft Skill' competency area. This included competencies that were: 'Public Speaking', 'Writing' and 'Personal Communication'. These are only included here to show how other competency areas may be considered and that the assessment need not necessarily be confined to technical competencies. Indeed, for this organisation, the soft skills were essential for all consultants, but these are not included in this book for the sake of brevity. The descriptions and indicators for each of these competencies are shown in Table 5.3.

Figure 5.3 The 'Skill' competency type for the company framework

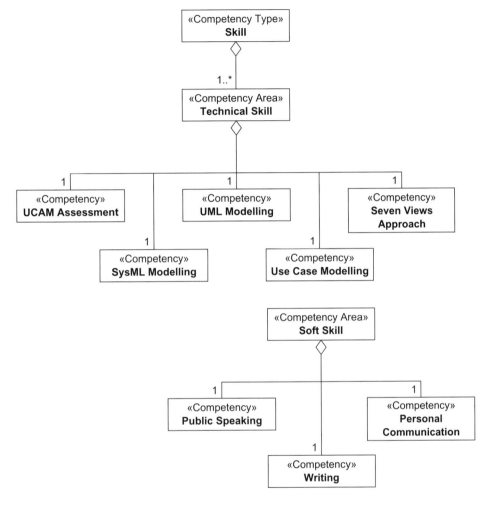

Table 5.3 Definition of level 1 indicators for the 'Skill' competency types

Competency	Description	Level 1 indicators
UML Modelling	This competency reflects the ability to use the UML	• Must hold the 'Modelling' competency • Is familiar with the background to UML • Is familiar with the ownership of UML

(Continued)

Table 5.3 *(Continued)*

Competency	Description	Level 1 indicators
		• Can name the six structural diagrams • Can name the seven behavioural diagrams • Understands the use of each of the structural diagrams • Understands the use of each of the behavioural diagrams • Understands the relationships between the diagrams • Understands the language extension mechanisms • Can explain what the UML meta-model is
SysML Modelling	This competency reflects the ability to use the SysML	• Must hold the 'Modelling' competency • Is familiar with the background to SysML • Is familiar with the ownership of SysML • Can name the five structural diagrams • Can name the four behavioural diagrams • Understands the use of each of the structural diagrams • Understands the use of each of the behavioural diagrams • Understands the relationships between the diagrams • Understands the language extension mechanisms
Seven Views Approach	This competency reflects the ability to use the Seven Views approach to process modelling	• Must hold the 'Process Modelling' Competency • Must understand the meta-model conceptual view and provide examples of its use • Must understand the realisation view of the meta-model • must understand the consistency relationships between the views • Must understand how each view may used • Must appreciate different tools and techniques that can be used to realise the views

(Continued)

Table 5.3 *(Continued)*

Competency	Description	Level 1 indicators
		• Must understand that the meta-model is tailorable • Must understand how the meta-model fits into the wider enterprise (such as life cycles, enterprise architecture, and so on)
UCAM Assessment	This competency reflects the ability to use the UCAM competency assessment model processes.	• Must hold the 'Competency Assessment' competency • Must understand the key concepts in UKSPEC • Must be familiar with at least one other external framework (for example, INCOSE, SFIA, and so on) • Must understand the UCAM meta-model • Must understand the 'Framework Definition' process • Must understand the 'Framework Population' process • Must understand the 'Assessment Set-up' Process • Must understand the 'Assessment Process' • Must be able to identify assessment criteria • Must understand competency scope versus competency profile • Must be able to suggest uses for competency output

So far, there has not been much difference between the definition of indicators in this bespoke framework compared to the source framework, but this similarity only exists at level 1, and there will be big differences at the remaining levels.

Level 1 – awareness

The main aim of this level is for the assessee to demonstrate that they possess the ability to 'speak knowledgeably about a particular aspect of the competency. The main aim is for the assessee to demonstrate that they understand each indicator fully, and back this up with examples – either theoretical or real-life'.

In terms of the topics about which the assessee must share their knowledge, this is defined by the key indicators shown in the previous tables.

Therefore, to obtain 'level 1 – awareness', in the 'Modelling' competency, the assessee must demonstrate that they: understand the need for modelling (first indicator), can provide an appropriate definition of modelling (second indicator), and so on for all the indicators.

Level 2 – support

The main goal of this level is for the assessee to demonstrate that they can 'reflect the ability to implement the concepts that were discussed at level 1 for this competency'. In this example, the indicators that are defined **apply** to the indicators that were **identified** in level 1. These indicators were defined as follows:

- Has achieved level 1, 'Awareness', for this competency. Therefore, for the 'Modelling Competency' the assessee must have met the criteria – they are able to demonstrate their knowledge – for the indicators specified.

- Has implemented the concepts discussed at level 1. Therefore, for the 'Modelling Competency', the assessee must have actually worked on a project where they have been able to: understand the need for modelling (first indicator), provide an appropriate definition of modelling (second indicator), and so on for all the indicators.

- Has been trained in some way. This is usually by a course or in some cases by on-the-job experience, in the areas described by the indicators at level 1. Therefore, for the 'Modelling Competency' the assessee must have actually been trained to: understand the need for modelling (first indicator), provide an appropriate definition of modelling (second indicator), and so on for all the indicators.

- Has supported other people in the implementation of work activities that use the indicators in Level 1. Therefore, for the 'Modelling Competency' the assessee must have supported people on a project where they have been able to: understand the need for modelling (first indicator), provide an appropriate definition of modelling (second indicator), and so on for all the indicators. Examples of this on a real project include: contributing to creation and generation of artefacts, participation in workshops, and so on.

- Has created artefacts related to the competency as characterised by the indicators for level 1. Therefore, for the 'Modelling Competency' the assessee must have produced, or contributed to the production of artefacts that demonstrate that they can: understand the need for modelling (first indicator), provide an appropriate definition of modelling (second indicator), and so on for all the indicators.

- Has controlled artefacts (applied version control, and so on) related to the competency as characterised by the indicators for level 1. Therefore, for the 'Modelling Competency' the assessee must have applied version control to artefacts that they have produced that demonstrate that they can: understand the need for modelling (first indicator), provide an appropriate definition of modelling (second indicator), and so on for all the indicators.

- Has had artefacts reviewed and has been able to address any issues that have arisen as a result of the review. Therefore, for the 'Modelling Competency' the assessee must have actually worked and had their artefacts reviewed by others where they can demonstrate that they: understand the need for modelling (first indicator), can provide an appropriate definition of modelling (second indicator) and so on for all the indicators.

- Can identify best practice in the competencies, such as standards, books, methodologies, etc. Therefore, for the 'Modelling Competency', the assessee must be able to reference best practice, techniques, approaches, standards and so on that demonstrate that they can: understand the need for modelling (first indicator), provide an appropriate definition of modelling (second indicator), and so on for all the indicators.

This list of level 2 indicators is then applied to all competencies in the competency assessment in exactly the same way. Therefore, when assessing against level 2 using this approach, there are never 'new' indicators that are introduced, just the same ones applied to all the competencies.

Level 3 – lead
The aim of this level is for the assessee to demonstrate that they can 'reflect the ability to be able to lead the activity that was described at level 1 and implemented at level 2'.

The company is heavily involved in consultancy work and they wanted to ensure that all of their consultants were suitably qualified and experienced; therefore, 'Level 3 – Lead', is the minimum requirement for a member of staff to be able to be considered as a consultant for the related competency.

In the same way that generic indicators were defined at level 2 which apply to all competencies, the same is done for level 3. These indicators are described as follows:

- Has achieved level 2, support. The assessee must have achieved level 2 and, therefore, level 1 (which was one of the level 2 indicators).

- Has led activity at a project level. Therefore, for the 'Modelling Competency' the assessee must be able to demonstrate that they have led a team or group of people where they have been able to: understand the need for modelling (first indicator), provide an appropriate definition of modelling (second indicator), and so on for all the indicators. Typically, the group that was led by the assessee would be made up of primarily level 2 people in the relevant competencies.

- Has supervised level 2 activity. Therefore, for the 'Modelling Competency' the assessee must have supervised people who are at level 2, where they can: understand the need for modelling (first indicator), provide an appropriate definition of modelling (second indicator), and so on for all the indicators. This supervision may be management supervision in the same group or may also include mentoring of level 2 people, perhaps from other groups in the business.

- Has managed level 2 activity (version control, release, setting work, assessing review responses, and so on). Therefore, for the 'Modelling Competency' the assessee must be able to demonstrate that they have been involved with assessing work, setting work, etc where they can: understand the need for modelling (first indicator), provide an appropriate definition of modelling (second indicator), and so on for all the indicators. Again, notice how the level of responsibility is increasing – at level 2 the assessee was required to have their work set and managed; at level 3 the assessee sits on the other side of the table and performs the setting of the work.

- Has formally reviewed artefacts. Therefore, for the 'Modelling Competency', the assessee must be able to demonstrate that they have reviewed artefacts on real projects where they: understand the need for modelling (first indicator), provide an appropriate definition of modelling (second indicator), and so on for all the indicators. Yet again, the level 3 assessee is now sitting across the table from the level 2 person and is performing the reviews.

- Has experience facing clients. Therefore, for the 'Modelling Competency', the assessee must be able to demonstrate that they can represent the organisation where they can: understand the need for modelling (first indicator), provide an appropriate definition of modelling (second indicator), and so on for all the indicators. This is the first indicator that reflects an outgoing image to the outside world, where the company's reputation may be at stake.

- Has some formal affiliation to a professional body, such as associate or full membership. Therefore, for the 'Modelling Competency' the assessee must be able to demonstrate that they have found the relevant professional body that relates to modelling and that shows that they can: understand the need for modelling (first indicator), provide an appropriate definition of modelling (second indicator), and so on for all the indicators.

Again, these level 3 indicators, like the level 2 indicators, are applied to all the competencies in the competency scope. Therefore, when assessing against level 3 using this approach, there are never 'new' indicators that are introduced; just the same ones applied to all the competencies.

Level 4 – expert
The aim of level 4 is for the assessee to demonstrate that they can 'reflect the ability to be a true, recognised expert in the field that is described by this competency'. In terms of a small company, such as the one in this case study, this will mean having an established reputation in the general field. This is for two reasons; the first would be that as the company is small, then being an expert in the company does not necessarily indicate general expertise in the field. If the company was larger and had, say, a thousand or more employees, being the company guru may qualify them for expert status. The second reason is that, due to the nature of the main work of the company, then being a recognised expert in the field is beneficial to the organisation.

The indicators for level 3 are as follows:

- Has achieved level 3, lead. This is similar to the criteria of both level 2 and level 3, each of which requires attainment of the previous level for qualification.

- Holds formal Chartered status from a recognised professional body. Therefore, for the 'Modelling Competency', the assessee must be able to demonstrate that they have found the relevant professional body that relates to modelling and shows that they can: understand the need for modelling (first indicator), provide an appropriate definition of modelling (second indicator), and so on for all the indicators. The assessee must hold the Chartered status qualification or equivalent.

- Has published in the field. This includes: books, first or second author on paper, first author on published public presentations. Therefore, for the 'Modelling Competency', the assessee must be able to demonstrate that they have published work that shows that they can: understand the need for modelling (first indicator), provide an appropriate definition of modelling (second indicator), and so on for all the indicators. Due to the size of the organisation, this will again mean publications in the public domain whereas for a large organisation, internal publications may, or may not, be considered.

- Has external recognition. This includes: speaking at public events, invited presentations, awards, panels, and so on. This is similar to the previous indicator but this time relates to oral communication, rather than written. Therefore, for the 'Modelling Competency' the assessee must be able to demonstrate that they have presented papers, spoken at events, and so on, showing that they can: understand the need for modelling (first indicator), provide an appropriate definition of modelling (second indicator), and so on for all the indicators.

- Has led activity at the strategic or programme level. Therefore, for the 'Modelling Competency' the assessee must be able to demonstrate that they can define process, policy, and so on that relates to modelling and that shows that they can: understand the need for modelling (first indicator), provide an appropriate definition of modelling (second indicator), and so on for all the indicators. At the expert level, the assessee must be seen to be driving the relevant disciplines forward both within and without the organisation.

- Has mentored level 2 and level 3 staff. Therefore, for the 'Modelling Competency', the assessee must be able to demonstrate that they have mentored staff in relation to modelling, showing that they can: understand the need for modelling (first indicator), provide an appropriate definition of modelling (second indicator), and so on for all the indicators. Notice again that the level of responsibility is increasing all the time and that the mentoring for this indicator applies to all levels below.

- Has contributed to best practice. This includes development of recognised methods, methodologies, tools, and so on. Therefore, for the 'Modelling

Competency', the assessee must be able to demonstrate that they have contributed to the knowledge pool showing that they can: understand the need for modelling (first indicator), provide an appropriate definition of modelling (second indicator), and so on for all the indicators.

- Is currently active in recognised professional bodies. Therefore, for the 'Modelling Competency', the assessee must be able to demonstrate that they have found the relevant professional body that relates to modelling and that they are actively involved in activities that show that they can: understand the need for modelling (first indicator), provide an appropriate definition of modelling (second indicator), and so on for all the indicators.

These indicators apply to all the indicators identified at level 1. Therefore, when assessing against level 4 using this approach, there are never 'new' indicators that are introduced – just the same ones applied to all the competencies.

The framework population process

The next process that was executed was the framework population process. The main aims of this process are to define the evidence types that will be acceptable for each level of competency and to define the applicable competency sets. This section will focus on defining the evidence types for each level.

Level 1 – awareness

The main goal of level 1 awareness is to 'speak knowledgeably about a particular aspect of the competency. The main aim is for the assessee to demonstrate that they understand each indicator fully, and back this up with examples – either theoretical or real-life'.

With this is mind, the following evidence types were defined:

- Tacit knowledge. This means that the assessee can talk knowledgably about the selected competency. It is important that the assessee can demonstrate that they truly understand the key concepts and is not just repeating something verbatim from a book or the Internet. This is an essential evidence type in that the level cannot be achieved without this being demonstrated. It was decided that there would be an indefinite timeliness set for this evidence type, providing of course that the assessee can answer questions successfully.

- Informal training course. This means that the assessee may have attended some form of training course or workshop related to the competency. This is an optional evidence type and is, therefore, not essential to gain this competency level. It was decided to attach a timeliness of two years to this evidence type. Therefore, for any course to be considered, it needs to have been attended in the last two years.

This level was deemed to be the minimum acceptable level for all competencies in the applicable competency set for all employees for this organisation.

Level 2 – support

The main goal of this level is for the assessee to demonstrate that they can 'reflect the ability to implement the concepts that were discussed at level 1 for this competency'.

With this in mind, the following evidence types were defined:

- Formal training course. This means that the assessee must have some training in the relevant area. The training course itself must be formally recognised by the company as being of sufficient quality to be deemed appropriate to gain the level. For example, a course from an accredited institution, a course provided by a professional body (with associated CPD, or equivalent, points), a course that has been specifically mapped to a relevant competency framework or a course that is recognised as contributing to professional qualification. This training must have taken place in the last five years.

- Activity – artefact. The assessee must be able to demonstrate that they have been involved with work activity in this area. The evidence that will be accepted is proof that they have been involved in creating an artefact by being a documented contributor. This must have taken place in the last two years.

- Activity – sworn statement. Activity on a project may also be demonstrated by having a formal statement from a level 3 or level 4 person to state that they have contributed to a project and met the requirements of level 2. This must have taken place in the last two years.

- Activity – formal review. It is also possible to demonstrate activity by having work formally reviewed. In this organisation, all work is formally reviewed by level 3 or level 4 personnel before it can be released. There is a formal process for this in the organisation; therefore, review artefacts are deemed as acceptable proof. This must have taken place in the last two years.

This level was deemed to be the minimum level for any staff to hold if they were to be involved with relevant work activities in this area.

Level 3 – lead

The aim of this level is for the assessee to demonstrate that they can 'reflect the ability to be able to lead the activity that was described at level 1 and implemented at level 2'.

With this in mind, the following evidence types were defined:

- Educational qualification. In order to achieve this level, it is necessary to hold a minimum qualification of a Master's degree in a related discipline. There is no time limit on when this qualification was held.

- Lead activity. The assessee must have led activity on a project which can be demonstrated by being the lead author of a relevant project artefact. This must have taken place in the last year.

- Reviewer. The assessee must have been a reviewer for an artefact on a project. This must have taken place in the last year.

This level was deemed to be the minimum level for any staff to hold if they are to hold the job title of, or call themselves, a consultant.

Level 4 – expert
The aim of level 4 is for the assessee to demonstrate that they can 'reflect the ability to be a true, recognised expert in the field that is described by this competency'.

With this in mind, the following evidence types were defined:

- Professional qualification. The assessee must have achieved formal Chartered status or higher. Nothing short of full, government-recognised chartered or fellow-status will count, and the awarding body must be an official government-recognised professional body.

- Publications. The assessee must have published work in a recognised format. This includes: writing books and peer-reviewed papers. Non-peer-reviewed papers, such as some conferences and (definitely) white papers will not be recognised.

- Public speaking. The assessee must have spoken publically on behalf of the organisation. This includes: conference presentations, invited talks, seminars, and so on.

- Activity definition. The assessee must have been directly responsible for the definition of company policy, process or approach.

This level was deemed to be the minimum level for any staff to hold if they are formally to represent the organisation in this area.

Discussion
The approach taken in this case study looks, at first glance, to be very similar to that taken in the source standard, but there are some fundamental differences. The basic structure of the framework has been fundamentally changed by defining level 1 indicators specific for each competency, whereas levels 2, 3 and 4 apply across all competencies.

This is an interesting approach as it is far closer to what is perceived as best practice in the process assessment world where there is a lot more experience and published success stories. This is partly due to the vast number of capability standards and techniques, but also because the whole area of capability and process, it may be argued, is more mature than that of competency and competency assessment. In a situation such as this, it seems logical to learn what we can from previous work.

Another advantage to this approach is that life is made much easier for the assessors. Once the level 1 indicators have been defined, then the questions for all other levels remain the same, which makes remembering all the content far simpler and greatly improves the fluidity and naturalness of the assessment interview.

In terms of the actual content of the indicators and their associated evidence types, what is presented here may seem, at first glance, a little draconian. However, it is important to bear in mind that this company prides itself on its reputation and demands that no one can question the professionalism of its consultants, hence the high standards.

The application of the UCAM processes to this organisation was deemed to be a major success. All of the original requirements were met and the UCAM processes are now used as part of their standard operating procedures. Also, after having applied the UCAM processes in the first instance just by using a PAPS (pen and paper system) approach, it was decided to investigate the use of automated tools to enhance the execution of the processes.

CASE STUDY 2 – EXECUTING THE ASSESSMENTS

Introduction to case study

The previous case study focused on the definition of a bespoke framework for a specific business. This section looks at another case study, but this time from the point of view of the assessments themselves. Therefore, the emphasis here is on the 'Assessment Set-up' and 'Assessment' processes in UCAM. The source framework to be used was, this time, to be a direct implementation of the INCOSE framework. This framework is deliberately chosen as it allows the readers to compare and contrast the approach taken between this case study and the previous one, where a bespoke framework based on INCOSE was used.

The company for this case study was, in contrast to the previous example, a large multi-national organisation with many thousands of employees. It was decided to run a pilot project where a number of people with different backgrounds would be assessed against the same scope in order to see how useful the frameworks and the processes would be to the business.

The first step was to understand why the company wanted to carry out the work in the first place. The basic requirements were as follows:

- to understand how competency could be used to help the general business in terms of internal assessments;
- to see if competency assessments could provide an 'edge' over competitors who may not use such an approach;
- to assess how useful one particular source framework is for the purposes of the main business.

With these in mind, it was decided to carry out the assessments on a small sample of systems engineers using the INCOSE framework. The UCAM processes were then executed.

The framework definition process

The first process that was executed as part of the whole UCAM assessment was the 'Framework Definition' process. In this case study, the INCOSE framework was identified by the company as being their source framework. The INCOSE framework model was used and then mapped onto the UCAM meta-model.

This has been covered in detail elsewhere in this book, so no further thought will be given to it at this point.

The framework population process

The framework population process is mainly concerned with defining the applicable competency set and the evidence types that are to be accepted as demonstration for the indicators. The applicable competency set was generated based on the roles that were to be assessed within the organisation. As this was an experimental assessment, it was decided that the definition of the applicable competency set did not need to be 100 per cent correct at this point as the results of this assessment exercise would then be used as an input to the main assessment programme. The applicable competency set was defined as being interested in the following competencies:

- Systems thinking – systems concepts. This competency covers the absolute fundamentals of systems engineering and was therefore seen as being an essential competency for all systems engineers.

- Systems thinking – super-system capability issues. Due to the nature of the work carried out by the company, it is important that the engineers can see the 'bigger picture' of the systems on which they work, therefore this competency was seen as being very important.

- Holistic life-cycle view – determine and manage stakeholder requirements. As with many systems engineering organisations, there is a great deal of import associated with getting the requirements of a project right; therefore, this was seen as an essential competency for all staff in the organisation.

- Holistic life-cycle view – systems integration and verification. Continuing from the last point, systems integration forms a large part of the company's work. Whenever systems are integrated, there is a great need for the various system elements to work together to form the overall systems, which highlights this competency as essential.

- Holistic life-cycle view – validation. This ensures that a system meets the original requirements – it does what it is supposed to do.

- Holistic life-cycle view – functional analysis. This covers the basics of functional analysis as applied to a system.

- Holistic life-cycle view – modelling and simulation. This covers modelling and simulation at the broadest level. As a point of interest, remember that in the previous case study, this competency was deemed to be too generic, and a whole set of other competencies was defined.

- Systems engineering management – life-cycle process definition. A key part of any systems engineering activity is to have a good approach in place. An essential part of any approach is a good process; therefore, all engineers must have at least an appreciation of the key processes and how they fit in the overall life cycles associated with projects, products and programmes.

- Systems engineering management – planning, monitoring and controlling. This covers basic project management principles. Again, for interest's sake, this single competency would map onto almost the whole of the APM framework.

These competencies form the applicable competency set. The applicable competency set is used as a basis for defining the competency scopes for each role in the organisation. These competencies will, therefore, form the horizontal axis of the competency scope, with the actual competency levels forming the vertical axis.

In terms of the evidence types that would be used at each level, there was a completely different approach taken to the one that was used in the previous case study. In that example, the evidence types were very well defined and the criteria for each indicator were very strict. In this example, the opposite approach was taken, in that the criteria were very loose. This was decided upon as this set of assessments was to be used as an input to a larger assessment programme. With this in mind, it was decided that very few evidence types would be defined and that the assessors would decide, on an assessment-by-assessment basis, what the appropriate criteria would be. In this way it would then be possible to abstract out a common set of criteria to be used at each level which would then form the definition of a more formal set of evidence types for future assessments.

The evidence types that were given to the assessors as guidance were simple:

- Level 1 – awareness: tacit knowledge, informal training course;

- Level 2 – supervised practitioner: formal course, activity;

- Level 3 – practitioner: educational qualification, lead activity;

- Level 4 – expert: professional qualification, publication and activity definition.

These evidence types should look familiar by now, as these are just the generic types that were introduced previously as a good starting point for thinking about evidence type definition. The explanations, therefore, for each one are kept to a minimum to avoid unnecessary duplication.

The resultant applicable competency set is shown in Figure 5.4.

Figure 5.4 shows the applicable competency (the themes and competencies taken from the INCOSE framework) set along the horizontal axis of the table and the levels up the vertical axis. The evidence types have been entered into each cell on the chart. Note that these evidence types are the same for each level; this would not happen when the definition is carried out more rigorously but, as this is being used as a starting point only, this is adequate.

Figure 5.4 The applicable competency set

Level	Generic applicable competency set								Evidence type
Expert	Professional qualification, publication, activity definition	Professional qualification, publication, activity definition	Professional qualification, publication, activity definition	Professional qualification, publication, activity definition	Professional qualification, publication, activity definition	Professional qualification, publication, activity definition	Professional qualification, publication, activity definition	Professional qualification, publication, activity definition	Professional qualification, publication, activity definition
Practitioner	Educational qualification, lead activity	Educational qualification, lead activity	Educational qualification, lead activity	Educational qualification, lead activity	Educational qualification, lead activity	Educational qualification, lead activity	Educational qualification, lead activity	Educational qualification, lead activity	Educational qualification, lead activity
Supervised practitioner	Formal course, activity	Formal course, activity	Formal course, activity	Formal course, activity	Formal course, activity	Formal course, activity	Formal course, activity	Formal course, activity	Formal course, activity
Awareness	Informal course, tacit knowledge	Informal course, tacit knowledge	Informal course, tacit knowledge	Informal course, tacit knowledge	Informal course, tacit knowledge	Informal course, tacit knowledge	Informal course, tacit knowledge	Informal course, tacit knowledge	Informal course, tacit knowledge
Theme	Systems thinking	Holistic life cycle view						Systems engineering management	
Competency	Systems concepts	Super-system capability issues	Determining and managing stakeholder requirements	Integration and verification	Validation	Functional analysis	Modelling and simulation	Life cycle process definition	Planning, monitoring and controlling

The assessment set-up process

The main aim of the assessment set-up process is to define a competency scope for each of the roles that is to be assessed. The roles that were decided upon were: requirements engineer, development manager, tutor and graduate. Each of these will be discussed in more detail along with their associated profile.

In order to generate the scopes for the assessments, it was important to look at what activities and responsibilities were associated for each role, but there were also some additional criteria. It is relatively easy to generate a scope based solely on the role, but it is also necessary to look at the context in which the assessment is taking place and to ask why the assessment is being carried out and what will happen to the results.

In terms of the rationale behind the assessment, there were several reasons identified as drivers for the assessment:

- to generate profiles for each member of staff that could then be used as a basis for placing consultants into client organisations;

- to identify gaps in staff competencies that can be used as a basis for generating a training programme to fill these gaps;

- to provide the company with a competitive edge when it comes to bidding and tendering for new work. As part of an industry shift towards looking for competent individuals, rather than just well-qualified individuals, some of the company's clients are starting to ask for competency profiles (the output of the assessment) as well as just CVs for staff that are to be included as part of the bid proposal.

With this in mind, the scopes were defined as discussed in the following sections.

The 'Requirements engineer' scope

Figure 5.5 shows the scope that was defined for the role of 'requirements engineer' in the organisation.

Figure 5.5 The competency scope for the 'requirements engineer' role

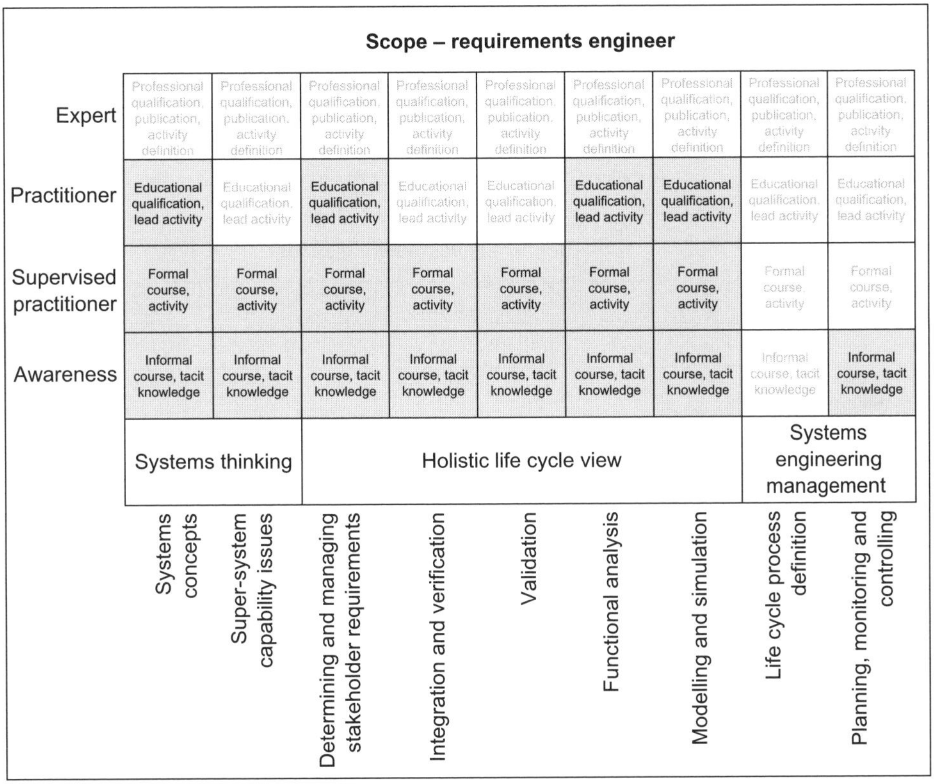

Figure 5.5 shows the competency scope for the requirements engineer role. The relevant levels for each of the competencies are shown by shading in the relevant cells.

There are some interesting features to this scope when the shape itself is considered. First of all, notice that it is not a 'flat' shape, but has highs and lows. The highest level on this scope is 'Level 3 – Practitioner' which is typical for most engineers. The areas in which the requirement for level 3 is present are related to the role name. Anyone who is involved in requirements engineering would be expected to have a good appreciation of systems engineering generally (the 'Systems thinking' themed competencies) and would be expected also to be at the same level for requirements-related life-cycle competencies. This includes 'Determine and managing stakeholder requirements' which is the obvious competency, but also two other competencies that require this high level are closely related: 'Functional analysis' and 'Modelling and simulation'.

Looking at the 'Systems engineering management' theme, there is an interesting pattern there also. Both 'Life cycle process definition' and 'Planning monitoring and controlling' are required competencies, but only at 'Level 1 – Awareness'. This is quite typical as the scope is asking that the individual understands management (level 1) but is not expecting any relevant experience in this area.

The 'Development manager' scope

Figure 5.6 shows the scope that was defined for the role of 'development manager' in the organisation.

Figure 5.6 The competency scope for the 'development manager' role

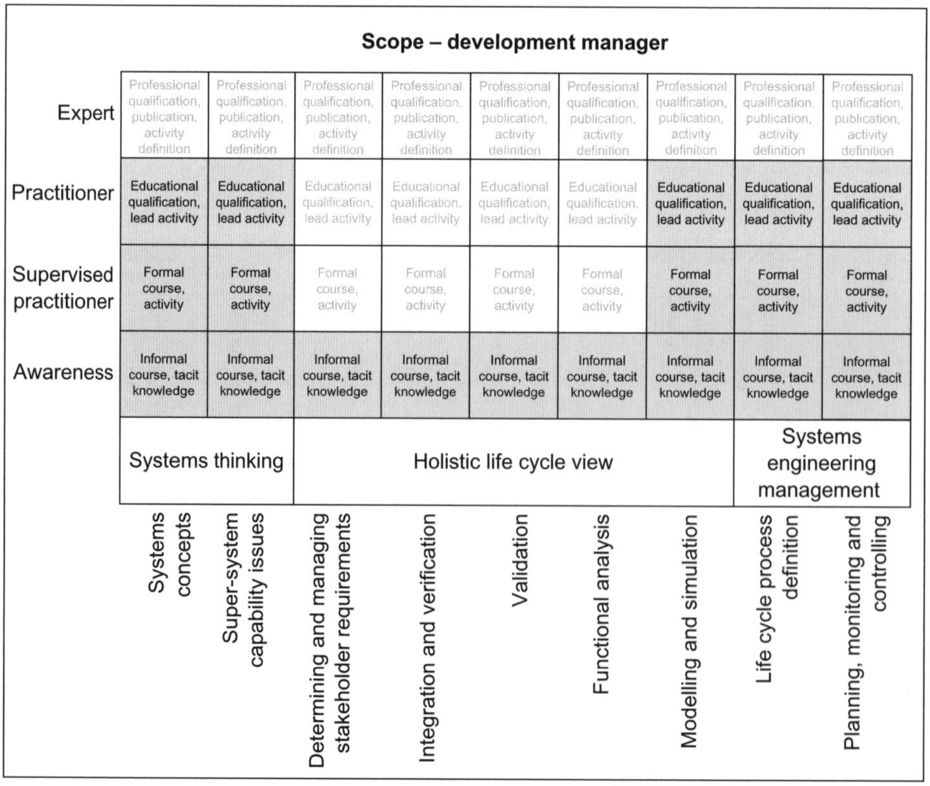

126

Figure 5.6 shows the competency scope for the development manager role. The relevant levels for each of the competencies are shown by shading the relevant cells. Notice that the same competencies are present, when compared to the requirements engineer scope, but this time the pattern is very different indeed. The 'Systems thinking' themed competencies are required at a high level in this scope, which is even higher than the requirements engineer scope. The life-cycle-related competencies here, however, are much lower, with four of them only being held at level 1. This is important, as it demonstrates that the engineers who may be performing the technical work (in this example, the requirements engineer) have far higher competencies in the relevant areas than the people who are managing them. This is completely normal and in some ways some aspects of these two scopes may be viewed as complementary. This is further demonstrated by the very high level required for the management-related competencies, whereas the more technical role only required level 1 for these.

One of the points made by the organisation during the discussion was that, in the past, there had been problems with managers who had little or no understanding of some of the technical concepts and, therefore, made them very inefficient managers. There was a definite requirement, therefore, that any manager **must** hold the 'Level 1 – Awareness' level in any area in which they are expecting to manage. Generally speaking, this is a very good piece of best practice.

The 'Tutor' scope
Figure 5.7 shows the scope that was defined for the role of 'tutor' in the organisation.

Figure 5.7 shows the competency scope for the tutor role. The relevant levels for each of the competencies are shown by shading the relevant cells. The scope here is really asking for a very high-level indeed in many areas. The reasoning behind this is that the competencies of the engineering staff in the company, bearing in mind that this is an engineering company, rely almost entirely on the knowledge and skills of the tutors who are responsible for training and mentoring staff.

This particular scope may look as if it is asking for the world, but bear in mind how crucial this role is for the company. Also bear in mind how few people could actually match a scope like this, and it goes to demonstrate that recruitment for such a role may take a long time indeed and that it may require looking for some-one with an established reputation in the relevant field.

Figure 5.7 The competency scope for the 'tutor' role

	Scope – tutor								
Expert	Professional qualification, publication, activity definition	Professional qualification, publication, activity definition	Professional qualification, publication, activity definition	Professional qualification, publication, activity definition	Professional qualification, publication, activity definition	Professional qualification, publication, activity definition	Professional qualification, publication, activity definition	Professional qualification, publication, activity definition	Professional qualification, publication, activity definition
Practitioner	Educational qualification, lead activity	Educational qualification, lead activity	Educational qualification, lead activity	Educational qualification, lead activity	Educational qualification, lead activity	Educational qualification, lead activity	Educational qualification, lead activity	Educational qualification, lead activity	Educational qualification, lead activity
Supervised practitioner	Formal course, activity	Formal course, activity	Formal course, activity	Formal course, activity	Formal course, activity	Formal course, activity	Formal course, activity	Formal course, activity	Formal course, activity
Awareness	Informal course, tacit knowledge	Informal course, tacit knowledge	Informal course, tacit knowledge	Informal course, tacit knowledge	Informal course, tacit knowledge	Informal course, tacit knowledge	Informal course, tacit knowledge	Informal course, tacit knowledge	Informal course, tacit knowledge
	Systems thinking		Holistic life cycle view					Systems engineering management	
	Systems concepts	Super-system capability issues	Determining and managing stakeholder requirements	Integration and verification	Validation	Functional analysis	Modelling and simulation	Life cycle process definition	Planning, monitoring and controlling

The 'Graduate' scope

Figure 5.8 shows the scope that was defined for the role of 'graduate' in the organisation.

The chart here shows the competency scope for the graduate role. The relevant levels for each of the competencies are shown by shading the relevant cells. The first thing that leaps out immediately with this scope is that there is not much in it at all. In fact, only three competencies have any level defined and these areas are all at 'level 1 – awareness'. The big question is – is it really worth defining such a simple and empty scope? In order to answer this question, first of all consider with what skills a graduate may leave a university. In most cases, it may be reasonable to expect them to be aware of what a system is, as the term 'system' appears in just about every discipline of science, engineering or any other for that matter. Also, every graduate would have been involved in some sort of final-year project where they would have been expected to manage their, or their team's, time and resources. Therefore, it is not unreasonable to ask for awareness of key management concepts.

Figure 5.8 The competency scope for the 'graduate' role

	Systems concepts	Super-system capability issues	Determining and managing stakeholder requirements	Integration and verification	Validation	Functional analysis	Modelling and simulation	Life cycle process definition	Planning, monitoring and controlling
Expert	Professional qualification, publication, activity definition	Professional qualification, publication, activity definition	Professional qualification, publication, activity definition	Professional qualification, publication, activity definition	Professional qualification, publication, activity definition	Professional qualification, publication, activity definition	Professional qualification, publication, activity definition	Professional qualification, publication, activity definition	Professional qualification, publication, activity definition
Practitioner	Educational qualification, lead activity	Educational qualification, lead activity	Educational qualification, lead activity	Educational qualification, lead activity	Educational qualification, lead activity	Educational qualification, lead activity	Educational qualification, lead activity	Educational qualification, lead activity	Educational qualification, lead activity
Supervised practitioner	Formal course, activity	Formal course, activity	Formal course, activity	Formal course, activity	Formal course, activity	Formal course, activity	Formal course, activity	Formal course, activity	Formal course, activity
Awareness	Informal course, tacit knowledge	Informal course, tacit knowledge	Informal course, tacit knowledge	Informal course, tacit knowledge	Informal course, tacit knowledge	Informal course, tacit knowledge	Informal course, tacit knowledge	Informal course, tacit knowledge	Informal course, tacit knowledge

Scope – graduate. Systems thinking | Holistic life cycle view | Systems engineering management

This scope as it stands may look fairly pointless but, as with all these scopes, it is only when they are compared to their associated competency profiles (the output of the assessments) that they really come into their own. In the case of the graduate scope, however, the real value starts to be added once more than one assessment has been performed, as this is when it is possible to see the trend of the competence of the individual or, to put it a better, to see the 'evolution' of the individual's competence – more on this later. Now that a number of competency scopes have been defined, it is possible to carry out the actual assessments, based on these scopes.

The 'Assessment' process

The fourth and final of the core UCAM processes to be performed was the 'Assessment' process where the actual assessments are carried out. Each of the assessments was concerned with seven competencies that were assessed to an average of level 3 (some were level 2 and 4, but the average is used as a general indication). On the basis of this, the time allocated for a single assessment was three hours, which would include the pre-assessment meeting, the assessment and the post-assessment meeting.

The pre-assessment meeting was where the two assessors met and briefly looked over the assessment scope and any information that was presented to them about the client. The roles of primary and secondary assessor were confirmed (in this case study, there was a set of assessors who could play either role) and the room readied for the actual assessment.

The assessment itself consisted of an informal interview where the two assessors, the primary and secondary assessor, asked leading questions that were geared towards exploring the assessee's knowledge of systems engineering, based on the competencies identified in the assessment scope. There are a few key points that had to be borne in mind when carrying out these assessments:

- The assessment should be non-intimidating and it should be stressed to the assessee that the assessment is not being carried out in order to catch them out or to expose gaps in their knowledge for any sinister reasons. Many people will view a competency assessment as a 'witch hunt' so must be treated with great care. Each assessee must be able to see the value, at least at a high level, of why the assessment is required. To this end, the first five minutes of the interview consisted of a brief introduction and the primary assessor would provide an overview of the assessment, the process and answer any initial questions from the assessee.

- The sessions were deliberately not run simply by reading through the INCOSE competency descriptions and asking a direct question for each level. This is a very unnatural way to establish a connection with a fellow human being and an important goal that must be strived for is to get the assessee to be open and honest about their competencies and achievements. For example, a leading question may be something like: 'Could you please tell me what "requirements" mean to you in your current role?', rather than: 'Do you know what a requirement is?', 'Are you able to identify stakeholders?', 'What is a quality requirement?' and so on. Indeed, people are far more likely to provide more information when the assessment is conducted as a general discussion, rather than an interrogation.

- Considering the two assessors, it is essential that the primary assessor has relevant competencies. For example, when using the INCOSE framework, it was decided that it was essential that the primary assessor holds at least a level 3 (practitioner) in all the 'systems thinking' competencies, level 3 of 'life-cycle process definition' and level 1 ('awareness') in all other relevant competencies. Indeed, a full competency scope for assessors has also been defined and this is an essential part of any assessment.

- Evidence was recorded by **both** assessors, who then compared their results at the end of the session and agreed on the final results.

An example of how the results were recorded is shown in Table 5.4.

Table 5.4 Example of recording the results of an assessment

Competency reference: 'System concepts', level 1				Rating scheme	
Indicator	**Evidence type**	**Evidence**	**Pass/ Fail**	**% range**	**Level rating**
Is aware of system life cycle	Informal course, tacit knowledge	Formal course certificate	Pass	81%–100%	Fully met
Is aware of hierarchy of systems	Informal course, tacit knowledge	No evidence	Fail	56%–80%	Largely met
Is aware of system context	Informal course, tacit knowledge	No evidence	Fail	**11%–55%**	**Partially met**
Is aware of interfaces	Informal course, tacit knowledge	Informal course certificate	Pass	0%–10%	Not met
		Rating %	**50%**		

The chart here shows the competency name and level at the top of the table. The left-hand column shows the indicators that are taken directly from the source framework. The second column shows the evidence types that were to be looked for by the assessors. As was discussed earlier, in this case study, these evidence types were kept to a minimum and much of the interpretation of results was left to the professional discretion of the assessors.

The third column is left blank on the form itself as this is where the evidence is recorded during the interview, shown here with the information already completed. The final column shows whether the assessor believes that the assessee has provided enough evidence to obtain a pass or fail for this indicator.

The 'Rating' section at the bottom of the table is a straight percentage of the pass or fail ratio that is used by the rating scheme to decide what level of competence is awarded. It was pointed out in the previous case study that the INCOSE framework is often inconsistent in the number of indicators defined for competencies, and here we can see an example of this. As there are only four indicators, then the only results possible are: 0 per cent, 25 per cent, 50 per cent, 75 per cent or 100 per cent. Due to this limited number of results, the difference between two competency grades (such as partially met and largely met) can be as little as a single indicator.

The example here shows that the assessee has achieved 50 per cent as their rating, which translates to an overall 'partially met' score for this competency at level 1 – clearly, this person has some room to improve.

Once the results have been recorded for each competency, at each level as specified in the competency scope, then the output can be collated into the competency profile. The competency profile (output) looks suspiciously like the competency scope (input) which is to be expected, but this time, each of the cells may be completed with the actual score achieved to provide the overall profile.

Figure 5.9 summarises the final profile. The basic table from the competency scope was used as the starting point and this time the evidence types are not shown as they were with the scope. The original competency scope is indicated by the border between the faded 'Not assessed' text cells and the other cells – any cells out of scope are marked with 'not assessed'. Any cells that are assessed are included in the scope and, therefore, have the score achieved written into the box ('Fully met', 'Largely met', 'Partially met' or 'Not met'). Any competencies that have scored 'Fully met' at a single level are shaded to increase the visual impact of the results. Any that have not achieved 'Fully met' have their score written into the box, which will be one of: 'Not met', 'Partially met' or 'Largely met'.

Figure 5.9 Assessment output (profile) for a defined role

	Scope – System Architect Role								
Expert	Not assessed	Not assessed	Not assessed	Not assessed	Not assessed	Not assessed	Not assessed	Not assessed	Not assessed
Practitioner	Largely met	Not assessed	Not assessed	Not assessed	Not assessed	Not assessed	Partially met	Not assessed	Not assessed
Supervised practitioner	Fully met	Fully met	Not met	Partially met	Not assessed	Not assessed	Fully met	Not assessed	Not assessed
Awareness	Fully met	Fully met	Partially met	Fully met	Fully met	Fully met	Fully met	Fully met	Fully met
	Systems thinking		Holistic life cycle view					Systems engineering management	
	Systems concepts	Super-system capability issues	Determining and managing stakeholder requirements	Integration and verification	Validation	Functional analysis	Modelling and simulation	Life cycle process definition	Planning, monitoring and controlling

Using the profiles

The profiles that were generated proved to be very useful in a number of ways – some expected and some not expected:

- The profiles were used immediately to place a consultant in a client organisation by matching the profile of the assessment against the original scope for a role. This was a predicted use of the profile.

- The profiles were used to generate a first step of a new training programme. This was achieved by looking where the largest gaps were between the profile (output) and the scope (input). In the example here, the largest gap appears in the 'Determining and Managing Stakeholder Requirements' competency. When all the profiles were considered together, they emerged as a common pattern for all assessees. On the basis of this, it was then possible to look into training options. This was a predicted use of the profile.

- One of the assessees, during the course of the discussion, stated that they did not hold chartered engineering status, despite having over 20 years of professional experience. When probed further, the assessee said that they were intimidated by the forms and all the necessary information that would need to be provided. The assessee was, therefore, delighted to discover that the results of the assessment could be used directly as evidence for gaining chartered status. This was a non-predicted and positive use of the profile.

- All assessees stated that they enjoyed the assessments and that, in all cases, they now knew more about both competency assessments and the INCOSE framework. This can be seen as actually raising the profile of INCOSE within industry: another unexpected and positive outcome.

- The final outcome was that this systems engineering manager now felt that he was in a position to make more use of the profiles as the assessments had been a great 'learning exercise'. This was seen as a valued contribution to future systems engineering best practice within the business and is intended to be used as an input to a higher-level approach to systems engineering, a part of which is concerned with systems engineering competency assessment.

Overall, the assessment was deemed to be a great success by the assessees, the assessors (naturally) and the sponsor of the work. Another outcome of the assessment was associated with assessing the suitability of the source framework, the INCOSE competencies framework, for use in the organisation.

Observations on the INCOSE framework

With regard to using the INCOSE framework, all the assessments that were carried out for this case study have been essential learning exercises, which can be used to further the use of the framework. It was always intended that any feedback would be gathered and then fed back to INCOSE and a few high-level observations are made here:

- Some of the competency descriptions are not very well balanced. For example, the 'determine and manage stakeholder requirements' competency has a total of 33 indicators across the four levels, whereas 'design for ...' has only 10 indicators. Also, two of the levels have only a single indicator assigned to each, resulting in possible scores of only 0 per cent or 100 per cent for each level. This has been discussed thoroughly in the previous two case studies.

- Many of the competencies cross-relate to one another and more work could be done in this area. For example, how does the competency for modelling relate to the competency for architecture design? Many of these competencies are very closely related and may well be dependent on one another. This is a feature that is present in the capability assessment world and one that could bear further investigation here.

- Some of the competencies don't really match their descriptions, such as 'life-cycle process definition', which relates mainly to the understanding of life cycles rather than processes. This can be misleading, particularly when the assessors are looking at headings as a basis for asking questions, as the results can be misleading.

It must be stated categorically, however, that the basic conclusion was that the INCOSE systems engineering competencies framework is an excellent tool for the systems engineering community and, although there are a few problems with it, this is natural for an evolving entity such as this framework. Indeed, these observations were fed back to INCOSE and, at the time of writing, there is another issue of the framework in the process of being released. Finally, bear in mind that comments such as these could be derived from assessments using any other framework.

CASE STUDY 3 – EDUCATIONAL FRAMEWORK

Introduction
The final case study departs from the previous two. Whereas the case studies presented so far have concentrated on technical-related competencies that were aimed at professional engineers, the final one has a very different target audience. The area of interest for this case study is education, in particular the assessment of schoolchildren and their performance over a school term. The approach taken to generate the following framework and associated assessments was exactly the approach described in this book – that of UCAM.

The background of this case study comes from the world of education and is mainly concerned with assessing schoolchildren during their education. Currently, teachers are required to produce a 'school report' card for each pupil that is updated at the end of every school term. These school report cards require that each pupil is given a rating, on a scale of between 0 and 4 (five levels in total) in a number of areas that have a single-word description, for example: 'Focus', 'Task completion' and so on. These single-word descriptions were grouped into three broad categories that were: 'Effort', 'Behaviour' and 'Attitude'.

At the time the work was started, the main problem was a perception that there was little guidance provided as to how to interpret these single-word statements, making assessment very difficult and unrepeatable from a teacher's point of view. Also, from the pupil's point of view, they had no real idea how they were being assessed, which meant that they did not know which aspects of their schooldays were being assessed at any point in time.

On an anecdotal level, there was also the idea that there was an imaginary 'line' that should not be crossed by pupils. Many people, including pupils, teachers and parents, used this concept of a line. Although this 'line' was a conceptual one, apparently some pupils knew when they had crossed it and were in trouble. Therefore, a secondary requirement of the exercise was actually to see if this 'line' could be defined in some way. This was to prove a challenging case study, but one that was sufficiently different to test fully the approach and core processes defined as part of UCAM.

Framework definition process

The framework definition process, in this case, used the school educational material as its starting point. There was no formal standard for pupil's competencies as such, but there was plenty of material made available to the teachers from the school and from the local education authorities, about what was expected. With this in mind, the following framework was generated.

Figure 5.10 shows that there is the key concept of a 'Competency' that describes the general skills required by each pupil. These competencies were grouped into three 'Competency Area(s)', each of which consisted of four 'Competency(ies)'.

The three 'Competency Area(s)' that were defined were:

- 'Effort', which describes how the pupil approaches a particular piece of work in terms of how much they are able to focus, understand and tackle work;

- 'Behaviour', which describes the way that the pupil interacts with fellow pupils, gets involved with lessons and their attitude towards equipment;

- 'Attitude', which describes their personal attitude in terms of the way they view themselves and their own responsibilities.

Figure 5.10 Framework definition for the educational framework

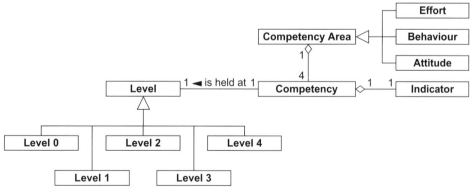

Each of these competency areas had four 'Competency(ies)' associated with it. The competencies that were identified for the 'Effort' competency area were:

- 'Focus', which describes how well a pupil can focus on a single task and relate this to other tasks and other interests in the outside world;

- 'Task Completion', which describes not only the pupil's attitude to getting work finished, but also assesses how well they can look back over their completed work and learn from what they have done;

- 'Problem Solving', which describes the pupil's attitude to how they tackle a particular problem, how and when they will seek help and how they work as part of a team to solve problems;

- 'Organisation', which covers areas as simple as having a tidy desk, up to organising their work within the wider context of the National Curriculum.

The competencies that were identified for the 'Behaviour' competency area were:

- 'Interaction with others', which is mainly concerned with the pupil's attitude towards others in the class and how their own behaviour may impact others;

- 'Behaviour decisions', which describes how much responsibility the pupils take based on their own behaviour, as well as assessing how they react to being instructed to behave in a particular way;

- 'Practical risk', which assesses how the pupil considers the impact of their behaviour in terms of personal and group safety, including equipment and tools;

- 'Class discussion', which describes the pupil's behaviour when holding a group discussion in a classroom environment, how willing they are to get involved and how much they contribute to the discussion.

The competencies that were identified for the 'Attitude' competency area were:

- 'Responsibility', which is the basic attitude towards learning and work;

- 'View of learning', which describes the pupil's attitude to the value of learning and how useful it is to their lives;

- 'Personal challenge', which is largely associated with assessing a pupil's motivation towards work and how they can set personal goals;

- 'Approach', which describes how the pupil's view their entire ethos on how they work, including their change motivations dependent on the subject matter.

Each one of these competencies is held at one of five 'Level(s)' that were defined as follows:

- Level 4 – excellent;
- Level 3 – good;
- Level 2 – satisfactory;
- Level 1 – poor;
- Level 0 – unacceptable.

For each competency, there was a single 'Indicator' defined in the form of a statement that could be applied to the pupil to which they could answer 'yes or no' or 'true or false'.

Framework population process

The framework population process is mainly concerned with defining the applicable competency set and defining the evidence type for the assessments. In terms of the applicable competency set, this is very straightforward as there is nothing to do. The applicable competency set is a subset of all the available competencies for assessment. In the case of this particular application, the competency set was created especially for the work at hand, therefore, it is the applicable competency set.

In terms of the evidence types that would be accepted and their associated timeliness, again this was quite straightforward. There are only two evidence types that need to be considered here:

- The observations of the teachers. As the assessment of a pupil is a very personal thing, it can only be carried out accurately based on the teacher's knowledge, understanding and personal relationship with the pupil. Therefore, the only evidence that can be accepted here for a third-party (teacher) assessment is the observation and opinion of the actual teacher. It could be argued that the results of academic and educational tests could also be used as an input, but this was discounted on the basis that test results are a different type of assessment altogether, and that the two sets of results, both test and assessment, should be used together to provide a complete picture of each pupil.

- The self-opinion of each pupil. This is only applicable in the case of a pupil performing a self-assessment, but it was seen to be a very good way to get pupils to understand the whole assessment process.

At this point, it is usual to look at the timeliness of each of these evidence types. Again, this is very simple as the timeliness is restricted to a single school term. This timeliness is the same for both evidence types.

The completed applicable competency set is shown in Table 5.5.

Table 5.5 Applicable competency set for the educational framework

EFFORT			
Level 4	Teacher observation, self-opinion	Teacher observation, self-opinion	Teacher observation, self-opinion	Teacher observation, self-opinion

(Continued)

Table 5.5 *(Continued)*

	EFFORT			
Level 3	Teacher observation, self-opinion	Teacher observation, self-opinion	Teacher observation, self-opinion	Teacher observation, self-opinion
Level 2	Teacher observation, self-opinion	Teacher observation, self-opinion	Teacher observation, self-opinion	Teacher observation, self-opinion
THE LINE!	*THE LINE!*	*THE LINE!*	*THE LINE!*	*THE LINE!*
Level 1	Teacher observation, self-opinion	Teacher observation, self-opinion	Teacher observation, self-opinion	Teacher observation, self-opinion
Level 0	Teacher observation, self-opinion	Teacher observation, self-opinion	Teacher observation, self-opinion	Teacher observation, self-opinion
	Focus	**Task Completion**	**Problem Solving**	**Organisation**

Table 5.5 shows the applicable competency set for the educational framework. In fact, this is not the complete applicable competency set, but just one-third of it as it only shows the 'Effort' competency area. This has been done purely for space-saving reasons as the evidence types are the same for each competency at each level, so there is little additional value in showing all the diagrams.

What is particularly interesting about this table, however, is the concept of 'the line'. The line here represents the boundary between what is acceptable and what isn't and provides a minimum performance level for all pupils. As will be seen in the next section, the way that the indicator statements above and below the line are treated is slightly different but, otherwise, the concept of 'the line' is a useful one that could be applied to any competency framework to show the minimum acceptable criteria for a competency profile.

Assessment set-up process
The assessment set-up process is concerned with defining the set of people to be assessed, which in this case was based on classes in the school. This is also the process where the assessment documentation is assembled and configured. Again, due to the simplicity of the previous framework population process, the documentation for this process is both simpler and easier to produce.

As there was only a single indicator defined for each competency at each level, it is actually possible to show these statements in the same format as the applicable competency set, with the indicator statements being printed in each cell, rather than the evidence types. This made the documentation far simpler and far easier on the eye than the usual volume of tables that is needed for assessments.

Tables 5.6, 5.7 and 5.8 show the assessment sheets that were generated.

Table 5.6 Assessment sheet for the 'Effort' competency area

EFFORT

Level 4	I sometimes spend time outside lessons following up subjects which have interested me	While completing a task I look for ways I can extend my understanding	I work with others to overcome problems together. I am specific about the help I need, and I work on other areas while waiting for help	My organisation extends beyond the specific lesson to include other areas of the curriculum and life
Level 3	I focus on what I have been asked to do throughout the lesson and attempt to link this to other things I am learning	I complete tasks, and think back over what I have learned without prompting	I listen carefully to any instructions and read information to see if I can find an answer before asking for help	My work is organised logically, and I tidy away anything which needs to go away
Level 2	I focus on achieving what I have been asked to do for most of the lesson	I always complete what has been asked of me	I make sure I know what my problem is before asking for help	My work is in my file and I always tidy my equipment away properly
THE LINE!	*THE LINE!*	*THE LINE!*	*THE LINE!*	*THE LINE!*
Level 1	I often only focus on a task when reminded by the teacher	I often don't completely finish a task, or I do the experiment but don't write down the results	I make some effort to understand what the problem is if I am stuck	I often lose work, and try to get away with not doing my share of the tidying up

(Continued)

Table 5.6 *(Continued)*

	EFFORT		
Level 0	I only focus on a task under one-to-one adult supervision and with threats	I only work under one-to-one adult supervision and with constant prompting	Immediately I encounter a problem, I 'down tools' and may become disruptive	I refuse to keep my own work together, or help to tidy up
	Focus	**Task Completion**	**Problem Solving**	**Organisation**

It can be seen here that the indicators are shown in the cells of the table. Each indicator is in the form of a statement that can be agreed with or disagreed with, making the assessment simple.

Table 5.7 Assessment sheet for the 'Behaviour' competency area

	BEHAVIOUR		
Level 4	The way I behave has a positive impact on those around me in terms of learning outcomes	I take full responsibility for my own effective behaviour	I work safely and accurately with full awareness of risk and help others to do the same	I act in ways which enable others to take part in discussions as well as contributing my ideas
Level 3	I always treat and think of others as I would wish to be treated myself	I choose behaviours which help me to learn (for example, listen carefully during class teaching)	I always work safely and effectively within a group	I listen carefully to everyone's views and think about the points which are being discussed
Level 2	I am polite to both adults and classmates	My behaviour does not stop others learning	I use equipment carefully and work safely round others	I mostly operate within the rules for class discussions

(Continued)

Table 5.7 *(Continued)*

BEHAVIOUR

	THE LINE!	THE LINE!	THE LINE!	THE LINE!	THE LINE!
Level 1	I sometimes say negative things about people (for example, people trying to learn are 'sad' or 'losers')	I usually wait for an adult to point out inappropriate behaviour before I control it	I behave thoughtlessly in ways which could be dangerous for others, or could damage equipment	I often thoughtlessly disrupt class discussions, by talking across others, for example	
Level 0	I am deliberately rude or aggressive to staff or pupils	If an adult asks me to behave in a particular way, I deliberately ignore them	I deliberately damage equipment and books and act dangerously around others	I deliberately interrupt discussions in a calculated and negative way	
	Interaction with others	**Behaviour decisions**	**Practical Risk**	**Class discussion**	

Again, the assessment sheet shown here has the same structure as the previous one, but this time Table 5.9 refers only to the 'Behaviour' competency area.

Table 5.8 Assessment sheet for the 'Attitude' competency area

ATTITUDE

Level 4	I take responsibility for progressing my own learning and try to help others as well	I apply lessons learned about learning to all areas of the curriculum	I like to challenge myself, and I know that if I do the best I can, I will always get a feeling of achievement	I look for an interesting way in to any topic I am offered and try to interest others as well

(Continued)

Table 5.8 *(Continued)*

ATTITUDE

Level 3	I work to improve the areas which will help me to learn	I have an open and enquiring mind and am ready to learn anything	I start with the idea that I will be able to complete a task, and I like the feeling I get when I have mastered something that was difficult	I feel tired at the end of a lesson, but I feel pleased that I have accomplished all that I can
Level 2	I accept that my attitude to what I am learning will affect the outcome	I am open to suggestions about how to improve my learning	I am more likely to persevere when I have a natural interest in the subject	I always make an attempt to understand a topic, but I make more effort for a topic I like
THE LINE!	*THE LINE!*	*THE LINE!*	*THE LINE!*	*THE LINE!* *THE LINE!*
Level 1	I don't feel like its my responsibility to change	I don't have a view of learning	I give up easily on a task and hope someone else will do it for me	I make little effort to understand what has been asked of me
Level 0	I blame my lack of progress on anyone or anything but myself	I argue that learning is worthless	I know I won't be able to do the task, so I refuse to try	I refuse to think about what I am supposed to be doing
	Responsibility	**View of learning**	**Personal Challenge**	**Approach**

Table 5.8 shows the final of the three competency assessment sheets that were produced. Again, the indicators take the form of a statement that has to be either agreed with or disagreed with, and this is where a subtle but important variation comes in. The assessment is carried out according to the following rules:

- In order to pass the assessment successfully, the pupils must answer in the negative for the 'Level 0' and 'Level 1' indicator statements. Therefore, when asked if the statement 'I blame my lack of progress on anyone or anything but myself' (Level 0, 'Responsibility'), then the pupil must answer 'no' rather than 'yes' to pass this level.

- In order to pass the assessment successfully the pupils must answer in the positive for the 'Level 2', 'Level 3' and 'Level 4' indicator statements. Therefore, when asked if the statement 'I accept that my attitude to what I am learning will affect the outcome' (Level 2, 'Responsibility'), then the pupil must answer 'yes' rather than 'no' to pass this level.

It is necessary for the pupil to achieve a pass in each level to achieve 'Level 4', which is the maximum.

Assessment process

The assessment sheets shown in the previous section were used as a basis for the actual assessments themselves. These assessments could be carried out relatively quickly, compared with the assessments in the previous sections. This was due to a number of reasons:

- There was only a single indicator per competency, making the whole process of assessment far quicker, as there was a fraction of the number of indicators when compared with the other case studies in this chapter.

- The answers to the indicator statements were based on the observations of the teachers and, because teachers spend a long time with their pupils, there is a very strong relationship between teacher and pupil, when compared to the assessors and assessees in the previous case studies. Indeed, in most cases, the assessors have never met the assessees before and have no previous or established relationship with them.

- Due to the high number of students in a group, it is quite easy for the teacher to remember all of the indicator statements, negating the need to wade through swathes of documentation, as in the previous case studies.

- Due to the simplicity of the assessment sheets, they could be very simply marked up during the assessments to produce the profile.

The profiles for the assessments would, therefore, look similar to the one shown below.

Table 5.9 represents a typical profile. This is a very powerful tool as it allows the teacher to see very quickly, with the use of 'the line', whether or not a pupil is on track with their studies. Also, by carrying out these assessments on a term-by-term basis, it is possible to see how the pupil's competencies have evolved over the school year and, indeed, over a number of school years. An additional benefit is that pupils were given these assessment sheets which gave them an insight as to how they would be assessed, which led to an increase in the morale of many of the pupils.

Table 5.9 Typical profile for the educational framework

EFFORT

	Focus	Task Completion	Problem Solving	Organisation
Level 4	I sometimes spend time outside lessons following up subjects which have interested me	While completing a task I look for ways I can extend my understanding	I work with others to overcome problems together. I am specific about the help I need, and I work on other areas while waiting for help	My organisation extends beyond the specific lesson to include other areas of the curriculum and life
Level 3	I focus on what I have been asked to do throughout the lesson and attempt to link this to other things I am learning	I complete tasks, and think back over what I have learned without prompting	I listen carefully to any instructions and read information to see if I can find an answer before asking for help	My work is organised logically, and I tidy away anything which needs to go away
Level 2	I focus on achieving what I have been asked to do for most of the lesson	I always complete what has been asked of me	I make sure I know what my problem is before asking for help	My work is in my file and I always tidy my equipment away properly
THE LINE!	*THE LINE!*	*THE LINE!*	*THE LINE!*	*THE LINE!* *THE LINE!*
Level 1	I often only focus on a task when reminded by the teacher	I often don't completely finish a task, or I do the experiment but don't write down the results	I make some effort to understand what the problem is if I am stuck	I often lose work, and try to get away with not doing my share of the tidying up
Level 0	I only focus on a task under one-to-one adult supervision and with threats	I only work under one-to-one adult supervision and with constant prompting	Immediately I encounter a problem, I 'down tools' and may become disruptive	I refuse to keep my own work together, or help to tidy up
	Focus	**Task Completion**	**Problem Solving**	**Organisation**

CONCLUSIONS

This chapter has presented three case studies with very different aims and outcomes:

- Case study 1, where a new competency framework was generated, based on an existing one, and used as the basis of the assessments. These assessments were aimed at the technical competencies of highly skilled professional engineers within an organisation;

- Case study 2, where a high number of people were assessed using an off-the-shelf competency framework as a basis for the assessments. These assessments were aimed at the technical competencies of a large number of engineers with varied backgrounds and skill levels;

- Case study 3, where a new competency framework was generated from scratch, based on many different information sources. These assessments were aimed at the general competencies of schoolchildren and were carried out by teachers.

The aim of this chapter has been twofold – to show how the UCAM approach can be used in the real world, but also to demonstrate the variety of domains to which the approach can be applied. The worlds of professional engineering and school education are poles apart, yet the same approach and the same processes proved effective in both cases.

Seeing the variety in these applications of UCAM will hopefully provide readers with the confidence and motivation required to try out some of these techniques for themselves. The approach can be applied in any domain and at any level of rigour. The processes shown in this book are also shown as guidance, so remember that they can be tailored for your own use. Above all, ensure that you add value to whatever you are doing by applying these techniques.

REFERENCES

Capability Maturity Model Integrated (CMMI) suite of documents, including: (2006) 'CMMI for Development, Version 1.2' (pdf). *CMMI-DEV (Version 1.2, August 2006)*. Carnegie Mellon University Software Engineering Institute. www.sei.cmu.edu/library/abstracts/reports/06tr008.cfm (Accessed February 2011).

(2007) 'CMMI for Acquisition, Version 1.2' (pdf). *CMMI-ACQ (Version 1.2, November 2007)*. Carnegie Mellon University Software Engineering Institute. www.sei.cmu.edu/library/abstracts/reports/07tr017.cfm (Accessed February 2011).

(2007) 'CMMI for Services, Version 1.2' (pdf). *CMMI-SVC (Version 1.2, February 2009)*. Carnegie Mellon University Software Engineering Institute. www.sei.cmu.edu/library/abstracts/reports/09tr001.cfm (Accessed February 2011).

Software Process Improvement and Capability dEtermination (SPICE). See ISO 15504 – Software process assessment suite of documents, parts 1 to 7 www.iso.org (Accessed February 2011).

INCOSE www.incose.org/ProductsPubs/products/competenciesframework.aspx (Accessed February 2011).

APPENDICES

APPENDIX A
A SEVEN VIEWS SUMMARY OF THE UCAM PROCESSES

INTRODUCTION

In Chapter 4 a number of diagrams were presented that described the requirements for the UCAM processes, the stakeholders involved, the processes and their behaviour and the artefacts and their relationships. As noted in that chapter, the diagrams were produced following an approach to process modelling informally known as the 'seven views' approach.

Following this introduction is a section that gives a **very** brief overview of each of the seven views. This is followed by a section that pulls together all of the UCAM process diagrams from Chapter 4, together with one additional diagram not found in that chapter, and presents them in sections corresponding to each of the seven views. No additional information is given on each diagram - this appendix simply acts as a convenient summary of the diagrams.

OVERVIEW OF THE SEVEN VIEWS APPROACH

The 'seven views' approach is a model-based technique for modelling business processes and is described fully in Holt (2009). It defines seven inter-related views of any process, and posits that the seven views are the minimum that are needed to ensure that a process, or set of processes, is both completely and consistently specified. The seven views and the relationships between them are shown in Figure A.1.

The diagram shows each of the seven views and also shows, using stereotypes (the words enclosed in angle brackets, for example, «use case diagram»), how each of the concepts described in the seven views approach may be realised using UML. It also shows how the seven views are related to the important concepts of the requirements for a group of processes (the 'Requirements Set' element in the diagram), the description of a set of processes (the 'Process Description' element) and the need to validate a group of processes (the 'Process Validation' element). Each of the seven views is **very** briefly described here.

Figure A.1 The Seven Views and their relationships

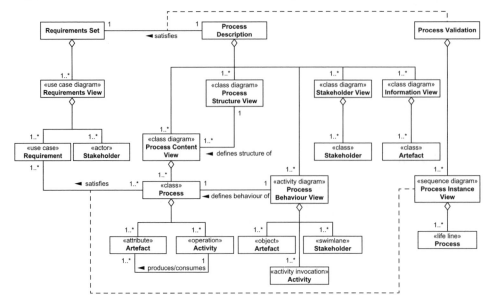

The Requirements View (RV)

The RV specifies the overall aims of a process or set of processes and can, if desired, be represented by more than one view. Often an RV is produced from the point of view of a particular stakeholder or group of stakeholders.

The RV is essential for validation of the processes to ensure that they continue to fulfil the needs of the organisation. Requirements for processes do change and so the Requirements View needs to be checked periodically to ensure that any changes to the requirements have been captured, allowing the processes to be changed, if necessary, to address the changed requirements. See Figure A.2 for an example.

The Stakeholder View (SV)

The SV identifies the stakeholder roles that have an interest in the processes being defined. It presents stakeholders in a classification hierarchy and allows additional relationships, such as managerial responsibility, to be added. The stakeholders appearing on the SV must be consistent with those shown on the RVs. See Figure A.3 for an example.

The Process Structure View (PSV)

The PSV specifies the structure of concepts and the terminology used when defining processes. For example, when one executes a process, does one carry out 'activities' or 'tasks' and are 'artefacts' or 'work products' generated. The PSV defines this vocabulary in order to ensure that consistency of terminology is used.

If many different processes have to be mapped to each other, then the PSVs for each set of processes form the basis for this process mapping, allowing the terminology used in one process model to be related to the terminology used in another. This is, effectively, what the UCAM 'Framework Definition' process is doing – relating the terminology and concepts for a competency framework to the generic assessment terminology and concepts contained in the UCAM meta-model. See Figure A.4 for an example.

The Process Content View (PCV)

The PCV identifies the processes available, showing the activities carried out and the artefacts produced and consumed. It may show general associations and dependencies between processes. It is important to understand that the PCV only **identifies** processes. It does **not** show how they are carried out. See Figures A.5–A.7 for examples.

The Process Behaviour Views (PBV)

The PBV shows how an individual process behaves and each process identified on the PCVs should have a PBV that defines its behaviour. A PBV shows the order of activities within a process, the flow of information through the process (that is, the flow of artefacts around the process) and the responsibilities, in terms of stakeholder roles, for carrying out the activities. See Figures A.8–A.11 for examples.

The activities and artefacts shown on a PBV must be consistent with those shown for the process on a PCV, and the stakeholder roles indicating responsibility must appear on both the SVs and RVs.

The Information Views (IV)

The IV identifies all the artefacts produced or consumed by a process, showing the relationships between them. IVs can be created at both a high or low level. High-level IVs simply identify artefacts and relationships, where low-level IVs show the detailed structure and content of individual artefacts. See Figures A.12–A.15 for examples.

The Process Instance Views (PIV)

The PIV shows instances of processes and the stakeholders involved in order to validate the processes by relating the execution of a sequence of processes back to the requirements for the processes. The PIVs along with the RVs ensure that the processes are fit for purpose and that all the requirements for the processes are met. See Figures A.16–A.18 for examples.

THE SEVEN VIEWS OF UCAM

The various UCAM process diagrams from Chapter 4 are presented in this section grouped according to which of the 'seven views' they are an example of.

The Requirements View (RV)

Figure A.2 The RV for the UCAM processes

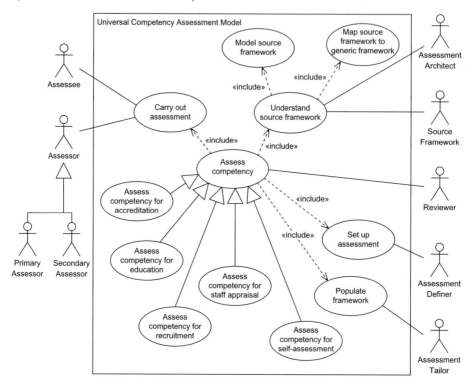

The Stakeholder View (SV)

Figure A.3 The SV for the UCAM processes

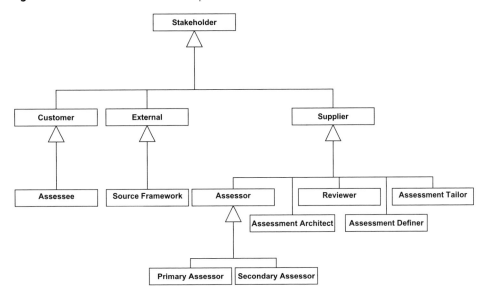

The Process Structure View (PSV)

Figure A.4 The PSV for the UCAM processes

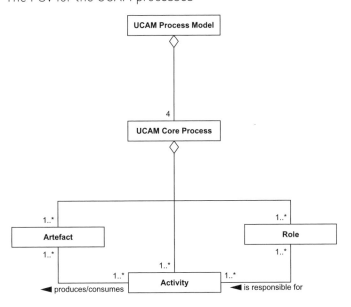

The Process Content View (PCV)

Figure A.5 The PCV for the UCAM processes

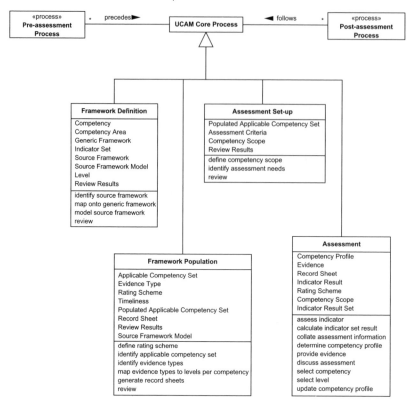

Figure A.6 Partial PCV for suggested Pre-assessment processes

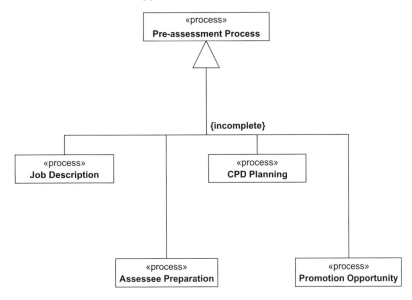

Figure A.7 Partial PCV for suggested Post-assessment processes

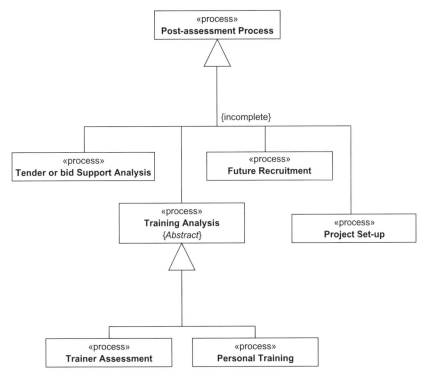

The Process Behaviour Views (PBVs)

Figure A.8 The PBV for the UCAM 'Framework Definition' process

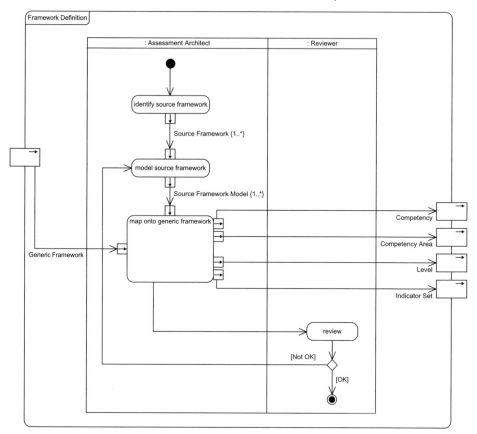

Figure A.9 The PBV for the UCAM 'Framework Population' process

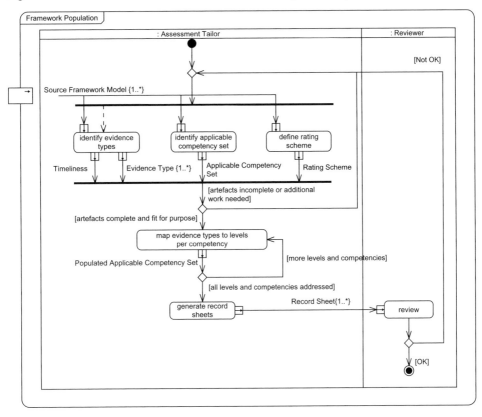

Figure A.10 The PBV for the UCAM 'Assessment Set-up' process

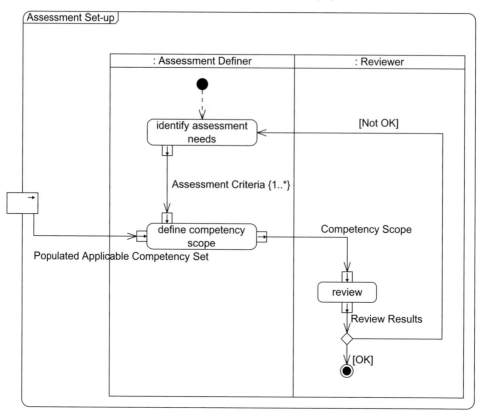

Figure A.11 The PBV for the UCAM 'Assessment' process

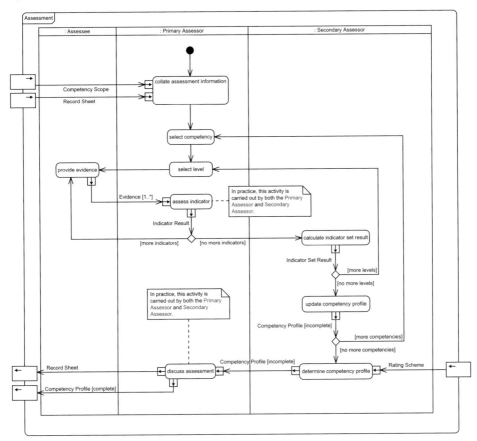

The Information Views (IVs)

Figure A.12 The IV for the UCAM 'Process Definition' process

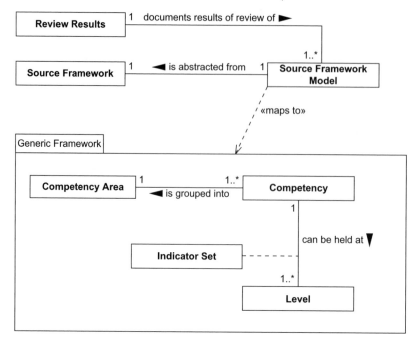

Figure A.13 The IV for the UCAM 'Framework Population' process

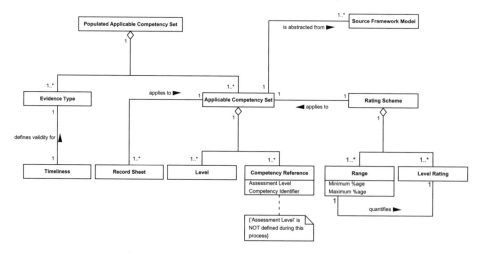

Figure A.14 The IV for the UCAM 'Assessment Set-up' process

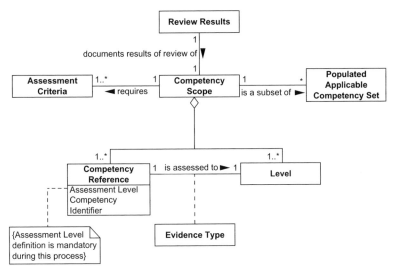

Figure A.15 The IV for the UCAM 'Assessment' process

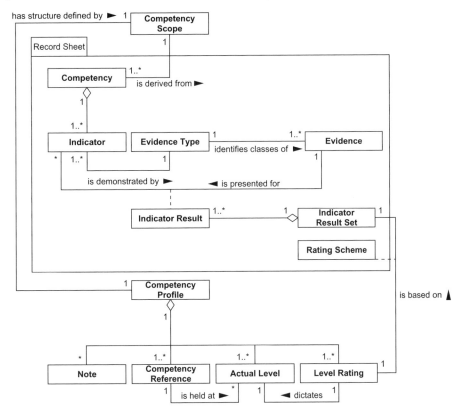

The Process Instance Views (PIVs)

Figure A.16 Example PIV for UCAM processes showing process execution for self-assessment

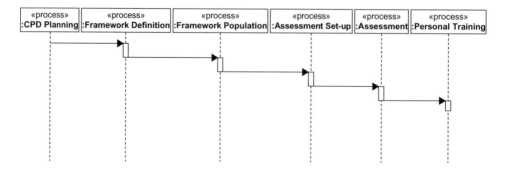

Figure A.17 Example PIV for UCAM processes showing process execution for recruitment

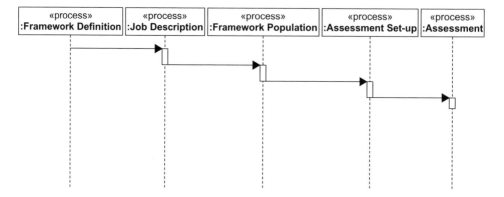

Figure A.18 Example PIV for UCAM processes showing process execution for appraisals

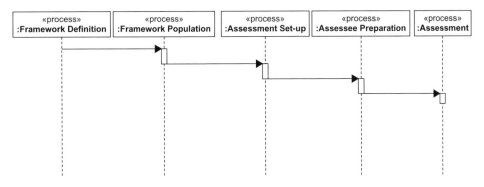

REFERENCES

Holt, J. (2009) *A pragmatic guide to business process modelling,* second edition. BCS, the Chartered Institute for IT, Swindon.

APPENDIX B
SUMMARY OF NOTATION

INTRODUCTION

This appendix provides a summary of the UML notation used throughout the book. Although the UML contains 13 different types of diagram, only four are used in this book. For each of these four UML diagram types two diagrams are given:

- the notation used on that diagram type;
- an example of that diagram type.

This appendix is **not** intended to be a tutorial on UML. For more information on the UML and the four diagrams used in this book see, for example, Holt (2009).

CLASS DIAGRAMS

Figure B.1 Graphical symbols for elements in a class diagram

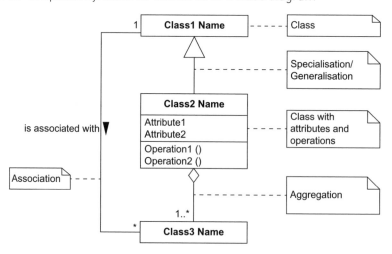

Figure B.1 shows the notation used on class diagrams. An example class diagram is shown in Figure B.2.

Figure B.2 Example class diagram

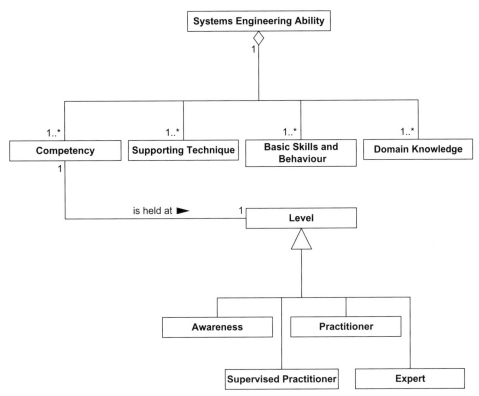

Figure B.2 shows that 'Systems Engineering Ability' is made up of one or more 'Competency(ies)', one or more 'Supporting Technique(s)', one or more 'Basic Skills and Behaviour(s)' and one or more 'Domain Knowledge(s)'. Each 'Competency' is held at a 'Level'. There are four types of 'Level': 'Awareness', 'Supervised Practitioner', 'Practitioner' and 'Expert'.

USE CASE DIAGRAMS

Figure B.3 Graphical symbols for elements in a use case diagram

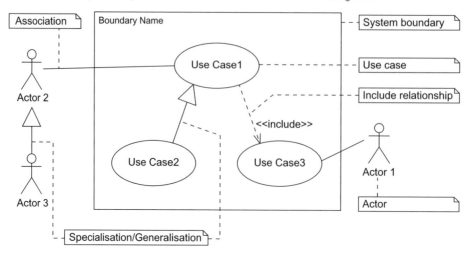

Figure B.3 shows the notation used on use case diagrams. An example use case diagram is shown in Figure B.4.

Figure B.4 shows the requirements (represented by use cases) and stakeholders (represented as actors) for UCAM (represented by the system boundary). The requirement to 'Assess Competency' includes the requirements to 'Carry out assessment', 'Understand source framework', 'Set up assessment' and 'populate framework'. There are many different variants of the requirement to 'Assess competency', such as 'Assess competency for accreditation', 'Assess competency for education', and so on. The stakeholders for the 'Carry out assessment' requirement are 'Assessee' and 'Assessor'. The 'Assessor' stakeholder has types 'Primary Assessor' and 'Secondary Assessor'.

Figure B.4 Example use case diagram

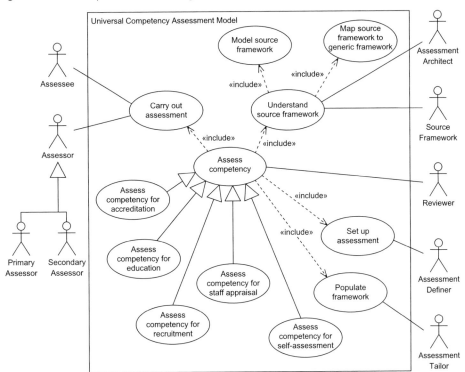

SEQUENCE DIAGRAMS

Figure B.5 Graphical symbols for elements in a sequence diagram

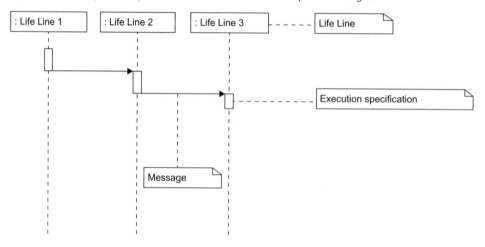

Figure B.5 shows the notation used in sequence diagrams. An example sequence diagram is shown in Figure B.6.

Figure B.6 Example sequence diagram

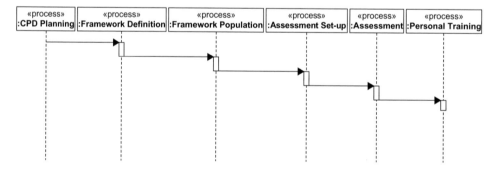

Figure B.6 shows a number of processes (represented as life lines) executed to fulfil a particular need (in this case, the UCAM processes that are executed in order to conduct self-assessment). Messages show one process ending and triggering the next.

ACTIVITY DIAGRAMS

Figure B.7 Graphical symbols for elements in an activity diagram

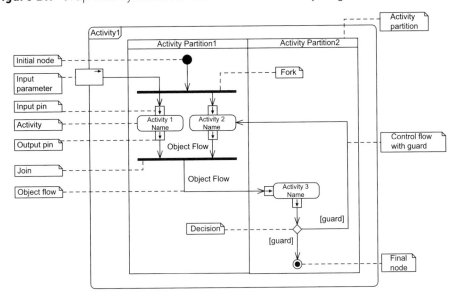

Figure B.7 shows the notation used in activity diagrams. An example activity diagram is shown in Figure B.8.

Figure B.8 Example activity diagram

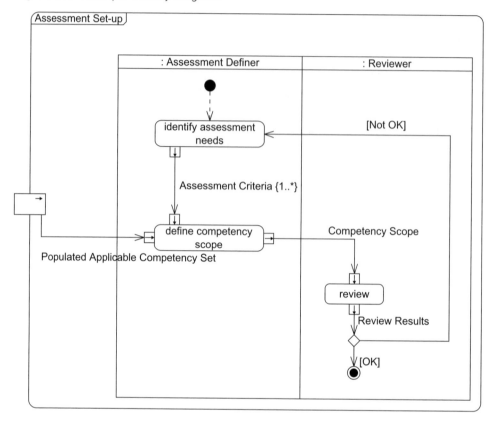

Figure B.8 shows the behaviour for 'Assessment Set-up' (one of the UCAM processes). Partitions are used to show that some of the activities are the responsibility of the 'Assessment Definer' and some of the 'Reviewer'. The input to the process (the 'Populated Applicable Competency Set') is shown as an input parameter. The artefacts that are produced by the various activities are shown as flowing between output and input pins on activities. A decision with two control flows that leave it controls exit from the process as indicated by the guards and the use of a final node.

REFERENCES

Holt, J. (2009) *A pragmatic guide to business process modelling,* second edition. BCS, the Chartered Institute for IT, Swindon.

INDEX